Dedicated to the late Pastor F. D. Robinson, my father in the gospel ministry, and to Drs. C. A. Pugh and Maynard P. Turner, Jr., all of whom worked long and tirelessly to teach me the science and art of the preparation and delivery of sermons.

84190

Additional Sermon Books
from Judson Press

Best Black Sermons, William M. Philpot, editor. Sermons that emphasize black dignity and proclaim God's power. 0-8170-0533

Outstanding Black Sermons, Vol. 2, Walter B. Hoard, editor. 0-8170-0832-2

Outstanding Black Sermons, Vol. 3, Milton E. Owens, Jr., editor. 0-8170-0973-6

Sermons from the Black Pulpit, Samuel D. Proctor and William D. Watley. Thirteen sermons that call for a renewed commitment to discipleship. 0-8170-1034-3

Sermons on Special Days: Preaching Through the Year in the Black Church, William D. Watley. Sixteen sermons for all celebrations of the Christian year. 0-8170-1089-0

Those Preaching Women, Ella Pearson Mitchell, editor. Fourteen sermons by black women that call Christians to develop positive attitudes and to find their identities by oneness in God. 0-8170-1073-4

Those Preaching Women, Vol. 2, Ella Pearson Mitchell, editor. More sermons by black women. 0-8170-1131-5

J. Alfred Smith, Sr., Editor

OUTSTANDING BLACK SERMONS

JUDSON PRESS®
Valley Forge

OUTSTANDING BLACK SERMONS

Copyright © 1976
Judson Press, Valley Forge, PA 19482-0851
Seventh Printing, 1990

Translations of the Bible quoted in this volume are as follows:

The Holy Bible, King James Version.

The Holy Bible, the Revised Standard Version of the Bible, copyrighted 1952 and 1971 by the Division of Christian Education of the National Council of the Churches of Christ in the United States of America. Used by permission.

The Bible: A New Translation by James Moffatt. Copyright 1954 by James Moffatt. By permission of Harper & Row, Publishers, Inc.

The Living Bible. Copyright 1971 by Tyndale House Publishers, Wheaton, Illinois. Used by permission.

The New Testament in Modern English, copyright © J. B. Phillips, 1958. Used by permission of The Macmillan Company and Geoffrey Bles, Ltd.

The New English Bible. © The Delegates of the Oxford University Press and The Syndics of the Cambridge University Press, 1961, 1970.

The Holy Bible, American Standard Version. Copyright, 1901, by Thomas Nelson & Sons. Copyright, 1929, by International Council of Religious Education.

Library of Congress Cataloging in Publication Data
Main entry under title:

Outstanding Black sermons.

Includes bibliographical references.
CONTENTS: Belk, L. S. The eyes of the Lord.—Blanford, C. The church and its mission.—Booth, L. V. The master dreamer.—Clark, E. M. How a people make history.—Gregory, H. C. The shepherd. [etc.]
1. Sermons, American-Negro authors. I. Smith, James Alfred.
BV4241.5.O9   252   76-2084
ISBN 0-8170-0664-8

The name JUDSON PRESS is registered as a trademark in the U.S. Patent Office. Printed in the U.S.A.

Contents

Introduction

Preaching in the Christian tradition has always proceeded from the presupposition that God has presented himself in history in the person of Jesus of Nazareth, and the primal purpose of that Presence is the elimination of estrangement between persons and God and between persons. That purpose is the basis of all preaching and the cornerstone of the gospel itself. However, the preaching posture in terms of content and style assumes many forms, as this collection of sermons reveals. The form is determined by myriad factors—the preacher's particular personality, his religious experience and intellectual pilgrimage, his world view, and his hermeneutical posture.

Preaching is, in essence, the telling of a love story, already told, for the plain purpose of reconciling persons to God and to one another. Its ultimate aim is to effect a holistic redemption which eventuates in that love which expresses and fulfills itself in justice. Admittedly, that is a big order for human hands. It is no wonder that Saint Paul declared, "We have this treasure in earthen vessels."

The preaching art is ineluctably molded and colored by the cultural context in which it takes place. Irrespective of its divine origin, it is contextual in character. Hence, there exists among Christians in America that brand of proclamation which can be rightly described as "black preaching." It is the very lifeblood of the black church, that peculiar community of believers in Jesus Christ brought together in history by blood, blackness, bondage, and the new birth. Black preaching is, without question, a unique religio-cultural phenomenon, unique because of the crucible of affliction out of which it comes. Prophets emerge only from "gap" situations: the gap between poverty and plenty, injustice and justice, war and peace, sin and righteousness. There is no need for a prophetic word in the absence of contradiction. The historic reality of existential dehumanization over against the recognition of essential dignity demands a word from the Lord. And that word of hope, deliverance, and liberation has reverberated in black churches across America all along the pathway of our pilgrimage.

One of the hallmarks of the black religious experience is a recognition of a natural synthesis of "sense and soul." In the corporate expression of the faith, fact and feeling are not seen as antithetical. Logic evinces feeling, and feeling is logical. The Word is worthy of being celebrated. And preaching-time is celebration-time. Preaching is the peak place in worship. It is the "Mount Zion" to which the pilgrims ascend and from which they descend. It is an event, a happening! The spoken Word is living drama, with the congregation participating as the supporting cast. Preaching is dialogue rather than monologue, and the mixture in terms of call and response makes for an experience that is more orchestral than antiphonal. A definite rhythmic quality marks the event, though the cadence varies from preacher to preacher. It is, therefore, utterly impossible to read the sermons of black preachers and experience even in a small way their import and impact. In the matter of delivery, there is a union of body and soul. The preaching act involves the total being. It is as nearly as possible a complete enactment of the divine encounter.

In addition to the synthesis of "sense" and "soul," and the dialogical nature of black preaching, much use is made of parallelism, an emphasis on experiences which parallel the great biblical events, such as Egyptian slavery, Babylonian captivity, Jesus' romance with the rejected, and God's ultimate balancing of the books. Herein lies the prophetic dimension of black preaching. In terms of linguistics, the message is transmitted in cryptic language replete with symbolism, imagery, and alliteration. A baptized imagination is appreciated and applauded.

One cardinal feature of the best preaching in the black tradition is the absence of inhibition with respect to speaking the truth. Freedom and fearlessness are expected from the pulpit. Timidity is scorned and despised. The preacher takes his cues from God and is expected to be the champion of the people's God-given rights and their God-appointed destiny.

The sermons which follow were born of a unique cultural condition, a predicament of pain which was and yet is. The prophetic thrust remains central due to continuing oppression. It shows no signs of diminishing. For as they say in Mozambique, "A luta continua"—"The struggle continues."

William Augustus Jones, Jr.,
Brooklyn, New York

7

Leotis Samuel Belk is the director of the Clergy Institute of Western New York in Buffalo, New York. Prior to taking this position he was the pastor of the Second Baptist Church of Le Roy, New York. He received degrees from Queens College, Flushing, New York; Virginia Union University, Richmond, Virginia; and the University of San Carlos, Guatemala, Central America. He also studied at Union Theological Seminary; the University of Guadalajara, Guadalajara, Mexico; Yale University; the Universities of Lagos, Ife, Ibadan, and Ghana, West Africa; and Temple University, where he is now a Ph.D. candidate. Among the many organizations of which he is a member are the Linguistic Society of America, the Society for Philosophy and Phenomenological Research, the American Academy of Religion, and the Society for the Scientific Study of Religion.

The Eyes of the Lord

Leotis Samuel Belk

Proverbs 15:3

Omnipresence

This means that God's eyes are over, in, and through the world; that there is no part of life, existence, or the world that God does not see. His existence might be called "eye-sistence." In fact, there is no "not" when it comes to God's "seeing." All negatives clear the deck at the sight of God. Because God sees all, life becomes fully possible. His seeing outsees the seeing of any other god, since some other god would have to see at least one thing that our God does not see. But since there is nothing that God does not see, there cannot be another god that sees what God does not see. And if there be another, it is useless because it is blind at least in one point. And if there be a god that sees as much as our God sees, it must be the same God, for our text says that God's eyes are in every place. Therefore, the God that sees all things in all places must himself be in all those places at once, ruling out the chance for another god to share the same spot with Him. And that which an eye that sees all does not see is simply and plainly—nothing. To be seen is to be something and to be somebody! Sartre relies heavily on this idea when he speaks of a man who is spotted in the act of looking through a keyhole. When the peeper looks up, he knows that he is completely at the mercy of his neighbor's eyes. He is both created and most definitely destroyed by the eyes of another.[1] If this is so for man, surely it is more so with God! God makes what he sees. Things come into being as they are seen by God. You remember that the world came into being when light fell upon it. The same thing happens inside a man's soul; wrote Paul Scherer:

> This earth of ours was finished millions upon millions of years ago. It circled round and round silently in the dark—inert, forgotten, dead; until something, groping its way through the blackness, found earth's face, and stayed, and played upon it. The light had come; and with it everything that

[1] William A. Luijpen, *Existential Phenomenology* (Pittsburgh: Duquesne University Press, 1960), pp. 195-197.

mattered came: color and beauty and life itself. So God, who once shone out of darkness, has in the face of Jesus Christ shone into my poor heart. The difference between that dead ball spinning in perpetual night, and this earth teeming with its wonders—that's the difference Christ has made for me.[2]

Light is the principal medium for eyes. Out of the dark and the depths God spun the light simply because his eyes are always full of light, and there is no darkness in them. What God sees, therefore, is what God makes and creates. Darkness and light are the same with God, not because he sees no darkness or sees no difference between darkness and light but because in every darkness his eye brings light.

God doesn't see just to be seeing, as if he were some television monitor roaming around the world. God's looking is not passive, detached, or disinterested. Wherever God looks—which is everywhere—God sheds light. For in him is light, and he is the light not only of men but also of stones and rocks, gnats and flies, alligators and rattlesnakes, fire and smoke, bacillus and capillaries, rubber bands and fabric—a thousand things. Our manufacturing things in the world does not change God's seeing what they are. If we would but reflect on it, we might find that God led us to our seeing.

> He that planted the ear, shall he not hear?
> He that formed the eye, shall he not see?
> (Psalm 94:9, KJV)

Ya can't hide

It's a fact that nothing can withdraw itself from God's eyes.

> Whither shall I go from thy Spirit?
>   Or whither shall I flee from thy presence?
> If I take the wings of the morning
>   and dwell in the uttermost parts of the sea,
> even there thy hand shall lead me.
> (Psalm 139:7, 9, 10*a*)

His hand leads because his eyes have already beheld our conditions. In my childhood in South Carolina, they used to sing: "My Lord's a writin' all de time, my Lord's a writin' all de time. He sees all you do, and he hears all you say. My Lord's a writin' all de time." "Ya can't hide. Ya can't hide. Ya can't hide 'cause ya don't know how." "God's got your number. He knows where you live. Death's got a warrant for you."

[2] Paul Scherer, *Love Is a Spendthrift* (New York: Harper & Row, Publishers, 1961), pp. 3-4.

Jesus, knowing that, could say when he spoke about prayer, ". . . Thy Father which seeth in secret shall reward thee openly" (Matthew 6:6, KJV). Amos, speaking of God wrote:

> Though they hide themselves in the top of Carmel, I will search and take them out thence; and though they be hid from my sight in the bottom of the sea, thence will I command the serpent, and he shall bite them (Amos 9:3, KJV).

It's an awful thing to fall into the hands of the Lord!

He sees and knows, Amos 9:3

That combination of God's seeing and knowing is a most potent combination for dealing with our lives and our behavior. If God saw and didn't know, we'd be like automatons in perpetual movement, doing everything for no reason. God not only sees us, but he also sees why we do what we do. That's why we say, "I see," meaning "I know." He *knows* me, the journey I pursue and the reason I go this way.

He sees and cares

His eyes are linked with his heart! What he sees, praise God, strikes some pity in his soul for me! How many people see and don't care! We see very well! We see the poor begging in the streets, but we don't care! We see the lonely, the forsaken, but we don't care. We see the weak, the oppressed, the sick, and the lost, but *we don't care! WE DON'T CARE!* How the conformities of our society rip apart seeing and caring, and carve feelings from faces, and plunge what joy there is into sorrow! But Jesus cares!

> O yes, he cares; I know he cares,
> His heart is touched with my grief;
> When the days are weary, the long nights dreary,
> I know my Savior cares.

He sees our sins

He sees our sinning and our failures, our sinking down, our unkindness, our love for our own conceits and deceits, our trailing behind our illusions—God sees our iniquity. He placed into the mouth of Isaiah these words: "Wash you, make you clean; put away the evil of your doings from before mine eyes . . ." (Isaiah 1:16, KJV).

But no man can put away one's doings, good or evil, from before the eyes of Jehovah. What he meant was "Stop doing it." Toss those intents, motives, egotisms, corroded loves away from you. Cast away that lust, that envy, that pride into the "sea of forgetfulness where it'll never rise again to condemn you at the Judgment bar." That "sea" is the place where God refuses to look. As he sees us, we can also "see" him—not in the same way he sees us, for we see through a natural eye. He sees through a supernatural eye. As the heavens are above the earth, so are his eyes, so is his seeing, so is the light which bursts forth from his eyes. We who take flights on the frontier between the infinite and the infinitesimal, who plunge into the ditches of disgust and soar to the singing of the seraphim—our double state, due to our disobedience in the Garden, has created for us a most peculiar double vision. We see, and yet we do not see. Our seeing is blurred. Our eyes are not fine-tuned enough. We think we see, but all that we see are illusions, phantasms, delusions, fantasies. We see wrong ideals, distorted images of ourselves and others. We fall from faith to folly, from resplendence to flicker! Those who refuse to see God's light shall be cast into outer darkness, and—from the view of this sermon—God shall desire to see them no more.

Judy, a girl from Philadelphia, told me about the time when her husband, Carl, died of cancer. She had said, "Carl, do you understand that you have cancer? Do you see what I'm talking about? Do you see?"

And Carl, leaning upon his pillow, started looking around the wall. "Yes, Judy, I see. I see Jesus coming along the wall, and he's coming over here to my pillow. Judy, do you see him? Do you see him?" he said, as light burned in his eyes!

"I am the light of the world," said Jesus. He is the light that lighteth every man that cometh into the world and, by implication, those hearts of light that goeth from the world. And now it becomes clear: Jesus is the light by which God has been looking at the world all the time. Throughout the life of our Savior we hear "Behold this!" and "Behold that!" Behold Zacchaeus in the tree, Bartimaeus in the crowd! He saw hearts—the hearts of the Pharisees when a man was let down through the roof of a house. He saw the centurion's faith. He saw the devils in people and cast them out! Jesus is the lens through which God sees the world and the optic nerve through which the world sees God. When a man takes Jesus into "the wings of his mind," the mind, the soul, the body—a man's whole being—"rightwises" itself; Jesus fine-tunes us. Slowly turning the dial of our little lives, Jesus tunes us from distortion to precision, from obscurity to clarity, from darkness to light—every new turn, every new light making the old light dull and the new light brighter—so that that old refrain is true: "Oh, how sweet it is to walk in the steps of the Savior, walking in the light, in the path of right! Oh, how sweet it is to walk!" Not a refrain but a certain verse says: "Amazing grace—how sweet . . . I . . . was blind, but now I see." Amazing eyes, how kind they look, that saved a wretch like me!

Now that we have become sons of God, we have also become lights of the world, cities set upon a hill that cannot be hid. We are lights of his light, light upon light, light through light, light with light. I say, "Shine, shine on in this world of darkness." You will not always see clearly while you shine. That's a strange paradox in "shining": we, unlike God, cannot know in full everything we see. But just because we don't understand everything we see doesn't make our shining any less bright. Here, we see through a glass "darkly," but one day we'll see him face to face. That means that one day it will all be as clear to us as the crystal sea beneath the throne of God. We'll see it clearly because we'll see the face of Jesus—finally, and at long last, we'll behold his face! Behold! We shall look at him! Behold, all ye nations of the earth! Behold, the Lamb of God that taketh away the sins of the world! Look at him, y'all! See! See! Get yourself an eyeful! His eyes are like flames of fire; watch and be ready. Sit down? No, no sitting down! Stand up and look! I got a whole eternity to sit down! Just this one long look will bring salvation, eternal life to win!

"For in the morning when I rise, he'll wipe the tears from my weeping eyes." Drying my tears—you hear that? After saving me without my deserving it, he takes special pains to wipe my weeping eyes! For he wants me to see without suffering, without sorrow, and without a sigh!

At the end, in those celestial portals of light, we must—and praise God we must!—join in with the four beasts around the throne, whose bodies are covered with eyes that look from north to south and east to west and everywhere in between. And we must join the wheel in the middle of the wheels that runs to and fro throughout the worlds with eyes in their rims, in untiring praise:

> "Holy, holy, holy is the Lord of hosts;
> the whole earth is full of his glory."
> (Isaiah 6:3)

Thus, I must close this sermon with a prayer:

Let the words of my mouth and the meditation of my heart be acceptable in thy sight, O Lord, my strength, and my redeemer! (Psalm 19:14, KJV).

Colvin Blanford is pastor of Christ Baptist Church of Gary, Indiana. In addition to his pastoral duties, he is a member of the Advisory Council of the Urban League of Northwest Indiana; vice-chairman, Board of Directors, Gary Opportunities Industrialization Center; chairman of the Education Task Force and chairman of the Subcommittee Task Force on Crime for the Interfaith Ministerial Leadership Alliance of Gary and Vicinity; and chairman of the Task Force on Crime for the Urban League. He also teaches "The History of the Black Church" at Indiana University Northwest. He received his Bachelor of Arts degree from San Francisco State College, his Bachelor of Divinity degree from Berkeley Baptist Divinity School; and his doctorate in religion and culture (Rel.D.) with an emphasis on social ethics at Southern California School of Theology, Claremont, California. He is a frequent speaker and lecturer at schools, colleges, and universities in California and Indiana.

The Church and Its Mission

Colvin Blanford

Matthew 28:19-20; 25:31-46

Before one can begin to address himself adequately to a discussion of the church and its mission, he must first come to grips with what the church is and what the church is not.

Contrary to the belief of some, the church is *not* an exclusive club but an inclusive fellowship. In other words, the church is not a closed society but an open fellowship. For at the heart of the church is the universal invitation, "Whosoever will, let him come."

Also, the church is *not* a "favored group." At the heart of the gospel is the affirmation that "God so loved the world" (see John 3:16, KJV) and that he "shows no partiality" (see Acts 10:34). Some of us have gotten confused because we have been referred to as "a chosen race" (see 1 Peter 2:9) or God's chosen people. But our chosenness does not mean that we have had conferred upon us some special honor in the sense of being "favored"; rather, it means that we have been chosen by God for service as a result of our accepting his invitation to be his servants in the service of mankind.

Furthermore, the church is *not* ours. We may have the title and deed to the physical edifice, but Christ and Christ alone has the title and deed to the spiritual body which is the living church. For it was he and he alone who said, "Upon this rock I will build *my* church" (see Matthew 16:18, KJV).

According to some interpretations, the church is not limited to those who make up the so-called "institutional church" but includes some who stand "outside" of this formal entity generally called the church. This interpretation is probably based, at least in part, on our Lord's reputed statement, "I have other sheep, that are not of this fold" (see John 10:16). On the one hand, this statement suggests that the sheep to which he is referring are *already his* but are simply not yet in "this fold." On the other hand, it may indicate to some that the sheep referred to are really "lost" sheep who must be "found" and brought into the "fold"—indicating that they are "potential" followers of Christ. Furthermore, some thinkers may interpret this statement to suggest or support the concept of ecumenicity.

Whatever the case, when this analogy is applied to the church, one comes into the "fold" by *choice* that is based upon *faith* through *grace.* Our faith expresses itself through accepting the Lordship and shepherding of Jesus Christ.

We would, therefore, like to affirm that whatever else the church is or is not, it is first and foremost the *family of God.* As such, one does not really "join" it but is "born" into it, for we still have the imperative of Jesus, "Ye must be *born* again" (see John 3:7, KJV). Furthermore, the church, as a *redeemed* and as a *redemptive* fellowship, is the *physical presence of Christ* in the world. The church, as the body of Christ, is a worshiping, witnessing, learning, serving, loving, obeying, growing fellowship. Moreover, the church is an *imperfect fellowship.* It is not made up of perfect individuals but of individuals who are *striving* for perfection. John tells us that "it does not yet appear what we shall be, but we know that when he appears we shall be like him (1 John 3:2*b*).

One's concept or understanding of the *mission* of the church reflects his concept or understanding of the *purpose* of the church. Purpose refers to that for which something is created or brought into being. It reflects aim, objective, intention. For example: a purpose of food is to nourish the body; a purpose of clothing is to cover the body; a purpose of water is to quench one's thirst; a purpose of brakes on a car is to stop the car; a purpose of gasoline is to propel a car; a purpose of the telephone is to receive and to transmit messages. The Greek word for purpose is *teleos.* Anselm used this concept as one of his intended "proofs" for the existence of God. He called it his "teleological argument"—an argument from effect to cause and from design to designer. The argument runs like this: if one sees a watch, one can rest assured that somewhere there was or is a watchmaker; if one sees a building, he knows that somewhere and at some time there must have been a builder; if one sees a baby, he knows that the baby must have had parents; if one sees a creation, he knows that there must be a creator. The church is a *purposeful* institution and organism because it has a *mission.* Basically, this mission or purpose is twofold.

On the one hand, the mission of the church is to *fulfill the Great Commission* by evangelizing the world. We are to spread the Good News that "God so loved the world that he gave his only Son, that whoever believes in him should not perish but have eternal life" (John 3:16). We are to spread the Good News that Jesus is the Christ, the

Son of the living God, that he is the Savior of the world, and that he wants to be Lord of our individual, corporate, and institutional lives. This Commission tells us that we are to "make disciples of all nations" (see Matthew 28:19). A disciple is a student, learner, or follower of someone else. To "make disciples" means that we are to win others to Christ by witnessing to the love of God *in* our lives and by demonstrating the love of God *through* our lives. We can do this individually, as did Andrew, as well as two-by-two, as did "the Seventy."

But, many of us have difficulty accepting our Christian responsibility to make disciples or be *disciplers.* Some of us are ashamed to witness publicly for Christ and to try consciously to win others for him. Therefore, we should ask God to empower us so with his Holy Spirit that we will become the disciplers that he wants us to be; for our Lord has said that if we are ashamed to own him before men, he will be ashamed to own us before his Father (see Mark 8:38). When one has been empowered by the Holy Spirit, he will have the kind of boldness that Peter had when he was willing to stand and boldly proclaim Christ crucified as the only power of God unto salvation. One will then even be able to say with Paul, "I am not ashamed of the gospel: it is the power of God for salvation to every one who has faith, to the Jew first and also to the Greek" (Romans 1:16).

As a matter of fact, some of us are "too proud" to be his witnesses. Many of us say that being a witness to the love of God as expressed through Jesus Christ is "beneath us." We say that trying to make disciples is "fanatical." As to the first statement, unfortunately, for some of us almost anything that Christ has said in Scripture for us to do is "beneath us." Therefore, we need to ask God for the kind of humility that will enable us to put *his* will before our own, to put *his* plan before our own, to put *his* purpose before our own. On the other hand, some people do become somewhat "fanatical" in their zeal. Many people try to "scare" or "force" people to become Christians. Still others go out "half-cocked" without really understanding *what* evangelism is about, *how* to do it, and the *spirit* in which one should do it. Evangelism is not merely going door-to-door handing out tracts. Evangelism (witnessing) *may include* these activities but is much *broader* and much *deeper* than just these. It includes how we "witness" in our interpersonal relationships in our business and professional activities, in our civic and social responsibility, in *all* of life! In everything we *think, say,* and *do,* we "witness" to our relationship to God through Christ. Therefore, we should try to reflect in our lives that Christ lives in *us,* hoping that others will see him in our lives and will invite him into theirs. Let us remember that we say more by what we *do* and how we *live* than merely by what we *say!* It is not merely a matter of asking people to follow Christ but showing people by *our* lives what it *means* to follow Christ. Our "words" *about Christ* must become "flesh" in the world!

The second part of the basic mission or purpose of the church is to *serve humanity.* In the twenty-eighth chapter of Matthew, our Lord plainly tells us that we should help meet general human need. His own life was dedicated to helping to meet the physical, mental, material, and spiritual needs of those with whom he came in contact. And he always started with people where they were. He would meet those needs that people *knew* they had before dealing with needs of which they were not aware. As his followers, as his representatives, as his servants, as his physical presence in the world, we should follow his example.

H. Richard Niebuhr has referred to the church as God's social pioneer. Norman Gottwald recognizes that other institutions and bodies are filling the role of servants to mankind and suggests that God sometimes utilizes people whom he refers to as the "crypto-church" as instruments of His will.[1] Nevertheless, the church *should* be God's *primary* serving institution, because the church is supposed to be concerned about and deal with *all* of life.

But one has to "feel" for the needs and concerns and problems of people before he can really become concerned to the extent that he is willing to help them to do something about their problems. This fact was driven home quite strongly to me when I saw (and saw again) the excellent musical play entitled *Don't Bother Me, I Can't Cope.* One of the songs was so poignant that it often goes through my mind. The name and central message of the song was "It Takes a Whole Lot of Human Feeling to Be a Human Being." Unfortunately, many of us don't function well as human beings in general or as Christians in particular, because we have either "suppressed" or "lost" our ability to "feel" for another human being. Paul was alluding to this kind of empathy when he encouraged us to weep with those who weep and rejoice with those who rejoice (see Romans 12:15).

I would not want to serve a God or have a religion which would

[1]Joseph M. Petulla, *Christian Political Theology* (Maryknoll, N.Y.: Orbis Books, 1972), pp. 172-173.

leave me devoid of feeling. Therefore, I am grateful that when the God of my faith touches one's life, one not only "feels" *him,* but he also develops empathetic "feeling" for *other people*—for their *needs,* for their *concerns,* for their *humiliation,* for their *problems,* for their *liberation,* for their *salvation*! Hence, the primary mission of the church is not singular but dual: *to serve humanity* in general, by helping to meet general human need, and *to fulfill the Great Commission* in particular, by helping to make disciples of all nations.

The words of Charles Wesley may help us to remember this twofold mission and purpose:

> A charge to keep I have,
> A God to glorify,
> Who gave His Son my soul to save,
> And fit it for the sky.
>
> To serve the present age,
> My calling to fulfill;
> O may it all my powers engage
> To do my Master's will!
>
> Arm me with jealous care,
> As in Thy sight to live;
> And oh, Thy servant, Lord, prepare
> A strict account to give!

L. Venchael Booth, now retired, was formerly pastor of the Zion Baptist Church of Cincinnati, Ohio. He received an A.B. degree from Alcorn A. & M. College in Lorman, Mississippi; a B.D. degree from Howard University School of Religion, Washington, D.C.; and an M.A. degree from University of Chicago Divinity School. He also received honorary degrees from Wilberforce University and Central State University, both in Wilberforce, Ohio; and Morehouse College, Atlanta, Georgia. He is very active in social and community services. Among many other activities he is the special secretary to the Ways and Means Department of the American Bible Society, a member of the Board of Directors of the University of Cincinnati, and one of the twelve vice-presidents of the Baptist World Alliance. He was very active in founding the Progressive National Baptist Convention, Inc., and has served as its vice-president, executive secretary, and president. He also served as the president of the Negro Sightless Society of Ohio and led the organization in securing a new home. He has written several religious songs and books and has received numerous honors and awards; he is listed in *Who's Who in America* and *Who's Who in the World* (3rd edition).

The Master Dreamer

L. Venchael Booth

And when they saw him afar off, even before he came near unto them,
they conspired against him to slay him.
And they said one to another, Behold, this dreamer cometh.
Come now therefore, and let us slay him, and cast him into some pit,
and we will say, Some evil beast hath devoured him: and we shall see
what will become of his dreams (Genesis 37:18-20, KJV).

But when they saw him coming, recognizing him in the distance,
they decided to kill him!
"Here comes that master-dreamer," they exclaimed. "Come on, let's
kill him and toss him into a well and tell father that a wild animal has
eaten him. Then we'll see what will become of all his dreams!" (Genesis
37:18-20, *The Living Bible*).

In the story of Joseph we see a composite picture of the plight of
humanity. In the world there have always been dreamers, but our
world has known few Master Dreamers. Joseph's father dreamed
dreams, very significant dreams, but they were not dreams that were
going to affect the world as vitally as did the dreams of Joseph.

Jacob's dreams dealt with his own problems of sin, conniving, and
deceit. One of his notable dreams was the one which came while he
was fleeing from his brother Esau's wrath—when he had a
remarkable vision, at Bethel, of a ladder reaching up to heaven; and
on that occasion a promise was made to him, similar to that which
God had given to Abraham on the same spot.

His next notable dream came when he feared revenge from his
brother Esau, who was coming to meet him with four hundred men.
The mind of Jacob was greatly agitated because he feared that the
meeting might be warlike. After dispatching a valuable present to
Esau and arranging his company in suitable order, he betook himself
to prayer. He spent the whole night wrestling with the angel of the
Lord, who appeared to him, and from whom he would not part unless
the angel agreed to bless him. In the course of his struggle his thigh
was disjointed; but Jacob, disabled in point of strength, resorted to
the spiritual weapons of prayer and supplication, and by these he
prevailed.

Then in the stream of history we come to the life of Joseph, one of the younger sons of Jacob. A remarkable combination of gifts and graces met in his character. He had the calmness, the shrewdness, the big-heartedness, and the faith of Abraham, along with the holy reverence and much of the gentleness of Isaac. He had the tender feelings of Jacob, without having his ruggedness and impetuosity. Brought early under the fear of God and thus taught to restrain those feelings which his brothers at times indulged in freely, Joseph soon became the object of their dislike. Their hatred was increased by his informing their father of their doings; and envy was added to hatred because of Jacob's undisguised favoritism. His frankness, perhaps his imprudence in narrating certain dreams which pointed to his being raised far above them one day, threw fuel on the flames of their jealousy.

I. Love Often Travels a Rugged Highway

Jacob loved Rachel and offered to serve seven years for the privilege to marry her. He wound up being deceived by her father Laban, who gave him Leah instead. This caused him to have to wait and work seven more years before he got Rachel.

Joseph was the son of his beloved Rachel, and so Jacob loved him, showed favoritism toward him, and gave him a coat of many colors. This coat plus his dreams were to cost him very dearly. He was thrown into a well, sold into slavery, and thrown into prison in a strange land. He was still the master-dreamer, and his dreams remained unchanged. Nobody could take away his dreams or the reality of them.

II. The Dreamer Who Could Not Resist Telling His Dreams

It was not enough to be the favorite son, to be spoiled and kept from hard work in the fields or caring for the sheep; he had to tell his dreams. He just could not keep them to himself. One night, Joseph had a dream and promptly reported the details to his brothers, causing even deeper hatred.

"Listen to this," he proudly announced. "We were out in the field binding sheaves, and my sheaf stood up, and your sheaves all gathered around it and bowed low before it!"

Then he had another dream and told it to his brothers. "Listen to my latest dream," he boasted. "The sun, moon, and eleven stars bowed low before me!" This time he told his father as well as his brothers; but his father rebuked him. "What is this?" he asked. "Shall I indeed, and your mother and brothers come and bow before you?" His brothers were fit to

22

be tied concerning this affair, but his father gave it quite a bit of thought and wondered what it all meant (Genesis 37:6-7, 9-11, *The Living Bible).*

One day, Joseph was told to go to see how his brothers were doing; this time they were twenty miles away. He went to Shechem and onward to Dothan. When they saw him afar off, they conspired against him: "Here comes that master-dreamer."

III. The Terrible Tragedy of Misunderstanding and Jealousy

There is a great fallacy in continuing to talk negatively with other people about a person whom you dislike. You begin to believe what you are saying. Others lend their weight to your prejudice. These brothers of Joseph communed too much among themselves. They saw the wide, open spaces around them, but they did not see the wideness of God's mercy. They felt the warmth of the soil beneath their feet, but they did not feel any nearness to the heart of God. They saw the stars above them, twinkling in the skies, but they did not see God, the Light of the World.

Jealousy blinds the eyes, darkens the soul, and kills the spirit of love. It is a tragic waste of time to envy another because of his talents, his treasure, or his good fortune. God is the giver of these things, and you have no control over them. These brothers had within their hearts the seeds of destruction and were destined to live with the heaviness of their guilt. They give us a classic example that whatever is done to hurt, hurts the "hurter" more than the one who is hurt.

IV. The Dreamer and the Dream Shall Be Satisfied

Man can kill the dreamer, but he can never kill the dream. (Martin Luther King, Jr., is a classic example.) We have lived to see it in our own time. We shall live to see it over and over again, if we live long enough. The jealousy of the brothers of Joseph did not change God's plan; they accelerated God's plan. Joseph needed to get to Egypt. He could not have made it so quickly had he not been sold into slavery. He needed to be in prison, but he would not have been there if Potiphar's wife had not lied. Joseph needed to interpret the dreams of the butler and the baker that he might also interpret the dream of Pharaoh.

When God is in the plan, there is no place that his servant can go that he does not go with him. God was with Joseph, the master-dreamer, and God will be with you, too. Go out into the world. God will take care of you!

Effie M. Clark, prior to retirement, was a lecturer in the Black Studies Department at California State University at Hayward, California. She was also a member of the Allen Temple Pastoral Staff in Oakland, California, having been ordained by the Alamo Black Clergy at the Church for Today in Berkeley. She earned a double major in philosophy and public speaking from the University of California in Berkeley, an M.A. in philosophy from Howard University, and a Master of Divinity and Master of Religious Education from Pacific School of Religion in Berkeley. She has been active in both teaching and planning black studies programs, including directing the Black Studies Interdisciplinary Planning Project under the joint auspices of Merritt College in Oakland, California, and Berkeley Unified School. She wrote the handbook entitled *African-American Curriculum, a Syllabus for Interdisciplinary Curriculum, Book 1, From Early Childhood Learning Levels to Grade 3,* which Merritt College published.

How a People Make History

Effie M. Clark

An enslaved people, an oppressed people cannot move toward liberating themselves until they first understand the nature of their oppression. But the opposite is also true. An oppressed people cannot understand the nature of their oppression before they are inspired with hope and a vision of the freedom that they desire.

To understand the nature of their oppression, a people must first know who they are; they must also know who their enemy is. They must organize themselves to struggle with their own weaknesses and the whole spectrum of their oppressed condition. It is at this point that such a people are no longer slaves; they are no longer dead to this world. As Brother Marcus Garvey said, "They now live a resurrected life."

They now shape their own destiny; they now determine the direction they should go, because they have entered into a renewed life. They now know themselves as a people, well on their way to becoming a nation.

Obviously, we as oppressed African people living in the captivity of America cannot shake off our mental shackles without leaders.

Let us look at the role of leaders to see how they are able to help people make their own history. Look at Moses in the Bible. He was born a Hebrew, but he grew up in the Pharaoh's palace as an "integrated" Hebrew. He was Hebrew, but he worked Egyptian; Moses thought Egyptian; he ate Egyptian and slept Egyptian.

But somehow Moses couldn't enjoy his privileged position as he looked from his palace windows and saw his people suffering under the yoke of slavery. When Moses' mother nursed him from infancy to childhood for the Pharaoh's daughter, Moses' mother told him who he was. So a spark was kindled in his heart for his people.

What Moses didn't know was that you can't be a friend to the enemy of your people and at the same time be a friend to your people. You can't be both. You can't serve two masters. It took a set of circumstances to teach Moses this lesson.

You know the story. One day, when Moses saw an overseer whipping a slave, Moses became so angry that he killed the overseer and buried him in the sand. A few days later, Moses saw the same slave whom he had befriended picking a fight with another slave. Moses went to them and said, "Hey, brothers, what's goin' on? You don't fight each other. We have to stick together."

The slave who started the fight replied, "Who do you think you are? Since when did you become a judge over us? You killed my overseer a few days ago. How do we know that you won't do the same to us?"

Moses had to make tracks and take flight from Egypt in order to escape execution by the Pharaoh. You see, the Hebrew slave didn't know where Moses was coming from. Moses hadn't really thought things out. He hadn't proved himself worthy to lead his people. He was ego-tripping. But when he got away from the scene, in a strange land among newfound friends, Moses took time to think things out. God then gave Moses insights into the nature of his people's oppression. And at the proper time God gave Moses the mandate to "free his people."

The first reality that Moses had to confront is that a people cannot free themselves so long as they worship the god of their oppressor. This usually means that in their hearts the oppressed fear their oppressor more than they fear God. The oppressor hovers over the slave with the army at his command. The oppressor controls the police; he controls the economic system. The oppressor decides when, where, and if he'll hire you. The oppressor makes all of the important decisions that affect your life. Indeed, the oppressor holds the power of life and death over you.

Now, it's easy to say that you don't worship whitey's god and whitey isn't your god. All that whitey really cares about is that you don't make him mad. If you do make him mad, you know and I know that if he wants to, he'll kill any one of us, especially when we appear not to accept our inferior status.

Flashing big naturals, wearing Afro clothes and dashikis, getting college degrees, and replacing the handkerchiefs and bandannas with attachés doesn't fool the white man, and the change of airs doesn't fool us either. An uncle is an uncle, and an auntie is an auntie—no matter what their hairstyles—unless their minds are hearts have been transformed.

The second reality that Moses had to face is that a people cannot stop worshiping the god of their oppressor unless they have a value system designed to meet their needs and their aspirations. They must have a set of laws to live by that will sustain them in their struggle to become unified and gain a true sense of direction. Thus, Moses was

26

equipped by God with ten basic laws to free the Hebrews' minds from slavish worship of their oppressor's gods.

The oppressor's laws are designed for one purpose only—to keep him on top, to keep him in power where he is, and, if anything, to make him more powerful. And if you live by the laws which the oppressor lays down for you to follow, you will continue to remain oppressed. That's why the oppressor always has two sets of laws, two different value systems: one set for himself and another set for the weak. He kids us along; he makes us think that one day, we'll be able to integrate with him.

The Hebrews had no land which they could call home. They were held captive in a foreign land. They were powerless. They were confused. They had no true sense of direction, for they were fragmented. They followed the leadership of their oppressor, who kept them scattered and confused.

Not until the Hebrews were marshaled together by a leader from their own ranks whom the God of their fathers had chosen did they become a people. Once they became a people, they began to make their own history. Before then, their back-breaking labor served only to contribute to the history of the Egyptians. While in bondage, the Hebrews had forgotten their God. While in bondage, the Hebrews got away from their roots. They tried to become part of somebody else's culture. The Hebrews were just messed up.

Once they rallied behind a leader with a vision—a leader who had received his mandate from the God of their fathers, a leader whose commitment to his people's liberation had been legitimated by the God of their fathers—the Hebrew people were able, through operational unity, to emerge from their wilderness wanderings with a sense of direction. They moved toward becoming a nation. They moved toward defining themselves in light of their roots, their heritage. They shook off the old slave name and defined themselves as the nation of Israel. The God of Israel saw their despicable and degrading predicament. The God of Israel intervened and led Israel, his bride, out of bondage.

Our oppression differs from the oppression of the Israelites in that we did not voluntarily migrate to these shores. We were ripped off our land in Africa. We were kidnapped and made slaves in Mother Africa and then brought here forcibly—in chains. We have struggled against our enslavement ever since we were brought here.

We've had leaders trying to help us raise our level of awareness and make us realize that our heritage, our history does not begin with our enslavement in America. Our ancestors in our mother country made world history. We must look to that heritage, which is our birthright, for lessons to be learned so that we won't make the same mistakes that put us in our present predicament. We must look at how other people, including our Mother Africa, made and are making their history, if we are to become a liberated people.

In 1791, a little African man in Haiti, Toussaint L'Ouverture, upset the course of Western history by uniting his people in a revolution against French oppressors. Toussaint L'Ouverture's defeat of Napoleon Bonaparte altered the history of the United States by giving the U.S. one less enemy to worry about. Things became so hot for Napoleon that he practically gave the Louisiana territory to the U.S.

Toussaint L'Ouverture struck such terrible fear in the white man's heart that the slave masters couldn't rest for fear that the slaves here would try to revolt. Toussaint made antislavery such a live issue that it would not go away. The slaves in the U.S. heard about that Haitian revolution. This knowledge gave the slaves here courage to struggle harder for their freedom and ours.

Mind you, forty years after the Haitian revolution, Nat Turner struck similar fear into the hearts of white Americans. Only thirty years later, they were forced to fight their battle to bring about unity against us. That battle was the Civil War. The Civil War came seventy years after the Haitian revolution. But the Civil War was not fought to free us. It was fought to unite white America in its history-making role as master over its collective destiny and over our destiny, too, as a people of inferior status, second-class citizens.

You know, we shouldn't argue with the white man when he assigns us a subordinate role in history (his story), for every contribution we have made to American history has been a contribution to his advancement over us. We cannot be both slave and free. We cannot increase the power of our oppressor without at the same time diminishing our strength. Why? Because he uses his power in support of his purposes and needs—not ours.

This very simple lesson was taught to us by Harriet Tubman. She wrestled with her condition until she came to a very clear understanding. She said,

I had reasoned dis out in my mind . . . there was one or two things I had a *right* to, liberty or death; if I could not have one, I would have the other; for no man should take me alive; I should fight for my liberty as long as my strength lasted, and when de time come for me to go, de Lord would let dem take me.[1]

Once Harriet understood this reality—that she could not be both slave and free—all indecision ceased; all confusion in her mind ceased. Harriet Tubman became unified within herself. And then her God, the God of her fathers, was able to counsel Harriet Tubman and guide her successfully in her commitment.

Harriet had to trust that there would be friends along the way to help her; but Harriet had to strike the blow against her enslavement and later that of her people. Harriet Tubman allowed herself to become an instrument for enabling us to make our own history commensurate with our aspirations, contrary to the will of our oppressors.

Once Harriet Tubman made the journey North by herself, she qualified to become a conductor on the Underground Railroad. She knew the road, she knew the dangers. She knew that you couldn't be overconfident about your friends' willingness to help you. You had to be careful not to push your friendship too far.

The slaves built legends around Harriet Tubman. They legitimated her as their hero. Before she stood up to her overseer as a slave girl, the family called her Minti. After she took her bold stand, they called her Harriet. After she began leading her people to the North on the Underground Train, the people called her Moses.

She notified the people of her presence by whistling like a whippoorwill, or hooting like an owl, or singing "The Chariot's Coming. . . ." When the slaves would say, "Moses been here," the slave masters wanted to know, "Who is this man, Moses?" The slaves smiled to themselves: our Moses is a *woman.*

Moses in the Bible made one trip out of Egypt, carrying all the Hebrew people with him. Harriet Tubman made nineteen trips into the South, carrying over three hundred people North.

Moses was well educated in the ways of the Egyptians. Harriet's education consisted of back-breaking labor as a field hand.

True, we are no longer chattel slaves; but we are caught up in a more insidious kind of slavery—that of half-free men. We are powerless. We lack economic and political power, two assets that every people must muster if they would be free.

[1]Lerone Bennett, Jr., *Before the Mayflower: A History of the Negro in America, 1619-1964,* rev. ed. (Baltimore: Penguin Books, 1964), p. 146.

We must extend our ministry and our commitment to the building of an economic base in our communities by establishing our own businesses and stores with mutual investments and mutually shared profits.

The Reverend Leon Sullivan, pastor of the Zion Baptist Church in Philadelphia, Pennsylvania, broadened his ministry to include stimulation of economic growth in the black community in Philadelphia. By his teaching the people in his congregation how to pool their seed monies together over a three-year period, they watched the interest on their savings triple so that they were able to buy first a multicomplex apartment building. Next, they built a million-dollar apartment garden complex, and three years later, they built on a four-acre site a 1.7 million-dollar shopping plaza, owned and operated by the African-Americans in Philadelphia.

Dr. Sullivan has this to say about the overriding importance of developing economic institutions in the black community:

> Black men must not only train for jobs but create jobs. . . . Our ultimate aim is to become involved in the full circle of national and international economics and affairs.
>
> This goal . . . means organization, discovery of the worth of capital, and knowing how to put a dollar to profitable use, attracting additional dollars and gaining additional purchasing power. As blood circulates in a body, keeping it warm, breathing and alive, so money must flow and flow, and circulate through and through the concentrated community, passing around and around in order to breathe life into it and provide new aspirations and opportunities for the young African-American population that is coming along. The aim is to keep some of the money at home instead of seeing it all flow out, week after week, into the suburbs, making the wealthy wealthier from the earnings of black folks.[2]

Unless and until we face the reality that we must build our own economic institutions, that we must build our own educational institutions, and that we must build our own social institutions—designing them to meet the expressed needs of our people—we have no right to complain about the white man's refusal to recognize us. His story (history) is made by his people. Anything we add to his story he incorporates into his story—if he wants to. Otherwise, our contribution goes ignored.

It is said that in the Japanese community a dollar goes through twenty-three hands before leaving that community. How many hands

[2]Leon H. Sullivan, *Build Brother Build* (Philadelphia: Macrae Smith Company, 1969), pp. 161-162.

does a dollar pass through in our community? African-Americans have a national income of over $41 billion a year; yet we own less than one-half percent (½%) of the business wealth in America!

Let me give you an example from our community: East 14th Street in East Oakland, California, is dying. Our sons and our daughters are forced to hustle an existence from this street. But what are we doing about it?

The transformation that would begin to occur in our East Oakland community would be great if a progressive church like ours would give its pastor a mandate to devote a considerable amount of his time to inspire the people of this community to pool their resources and plan a long-range program designed to revitalize East Oakland.

If our pastor's special gift lies in inspiring and bringing together business people who in turn will pool their skills/resources and develop corporate leadership with a sound, cooperative community base, we should permit him to develop that talent. To allow our pastor to do this under the aegis of our church is: black people making our own history.

Brothers and Sisters, we are in the community. The black community is in us and of us. There can be no separation among ourselves. *We are one people.*

With all the talented people and resources that are available to our community, there is no reason why we cannot reassess our commitment in light of twenty-first-century realities which we must anticipate if we are to deal righteously with the realities confronting us in this twentieth century. We must organize our community in the area of business. We must organize our community in the area of politics. We must organize our community in the area of religion. We must organize our community in the area of education so that our community can make our leaders accountable to us for their deeds. We must begin to take ourselves seriously enough to demand responsible leadership. And in order for that leadership to be responsible to us, we must legitimize it; we must be responsive to our leaders so that our leaders may draw from us strength and a true sense of direction.

People outside the African-American community must not be permitted to speak for us—revolutionaries or no revolutionaries. This is not going to stop by tomorrow morning, because we've let it go on for too long. The only way we can stop it is to muster enough group strength amongst ourselves so as to direct our own lives; we

31

must muster enough group strength to speak forcefully for ourselves.

Our Malcolm Xs, our Martin Luther Kings, our Marcus Fosters are ripped off without fear of reprisal from us because we are weak. We are powerless. Consequently, in our frustrations we do our in-group fighting in the presence of anybody and everybody, not realizing that we are setting ourselves up for a rip-off. Not that the rip-offs will not occur no matter what we do, but we must muster enough show of strength so that the enemy will think twice about sure consequences that will follow if he commits his dastardly deed.

We must come out of our wilderness wanderings and confusion, as the poet says:

> . . . walking blindly, spreading joy, losing time being lazy, sleeping when hungry, shouting when burdened, drinking when hopeless, tied and shackled and tangled among ourselves by the unseen creatures who tower over us omnisciently and laugh;
>
> . . . blundering and groping and floundering in the dark of churches and schools and clubs and societies, associations, and councils, and committees, and conventions, distressed and disturbed and deceived and devoured by money-hungry, glory-craving leeches, preyed on by facile force of state and fad and novelty, by false prophet and holy believer.[3]

As we put behind us our wilderness wanderings, the poet, Margaret Walker, lays upon us this challenge:

> Let a new earth rise. Let another world be born. Let a bloody peace be written in the sky. Let a second generation full of courage issue forth; let a people loving freedom come to growth. Let a beauty full of healing and a strength of final clenching be the pulsing in our spirits and our blood. Let the martial songs be written, let the dirges disappear. Let a race of men now rise and take control.[4]

[3]Margaret Walker, *For My People* (New Haven: Yale University Press, 1942), p. 14.
[4]*Ibid.*

Prior to his death, Henry C. Gregory III was the senior minister of the Shiloh Baptist Church in Washington, D.C. Before that, he was the pastor of the Fifth Street Baptist Church in Richmond, Virginia. During that time, he was also the university pastor of Virginia Union University, Richmond, Virginia, and was a faculty member in the Graduate School at the Theological Center. He held degrees from Howard University, Washington, D.C.; Drew University, Madison, New Jersey; and Harvard University, Cambridge, Massachusetts. During his lifetime he did graduate studies at Oxford University, England, and had many responsibilities, including chairman of the Theological Commission of the National Baptist Convention, U.S.A., Inc.; member of the Board of Trustees of the Legal Aid Society; member of the Board of Directors of the District of Columbia Society for Crippled Children; and member of the Citizens Advisory Council to the Superintendent of Public Schools of the District of Columbia. He frequently spoke to church, school, and community groups in many parts of the country and contributed many articles to religious periodicals.

The Shepherd

Henry C. Gregory III

In the picture gallery of humanity there hangs on the gripping wall of history a portrait of the good shepherd. Deep in the distant ages it is rooted, and each age and race has contributed perfecting strokes. Even Egypt, unimpressed by the shepherd's craft, added its concept of an ideal leader as a shepherd of the people who, when his herds are few, spends the day gathering them together. But it was with Israel that the portrait took its deathless and breathtaking shape. When Jesus of Nazareth came, winning the applause and attracting the admiring gazes of men, he picked up the title "shepherd" and wore it as a well-fitting garment. He adorned it without dashing its meaning. He made it luminous without rending its tissue. He took it with him through the gates of glory without emptying it of its sweet, human significance. "I am," said he, "the good shepherd" (see John 10:11, 14).

I. A metaphorical meaning

History suggests three aspects of shepherding to us. It is first of all a lowly estate. Martin Luther called it a "mean job, low-down work." It was the kind of job that no one wanted. Cervantes in his novel *Don Quixote* refers to the scholar and the shepherd as the wise man and the fool, respectively.

Secondly, shepherding is lonely work. There are different kinds of loneliness. There is the loneliness of displacement in which one is out of his natural habitat. A New Yorker may be with people in Stafford County, Virginia, and still feel lonely. The farmer may be on a crowded street in Chicago and feel very much alone. It was the loneliness of displacement that the psalmist experienced when he said, "I am like a pelican of the wilderness: I am like an owl of the desert" (Psalm 102:6). Then, there is the loneliness of abandonment and insignificance when one feels deserted by human sympathy and empathy; this was the experience of the Ancient Mariner when he cried,

Alone, alone, all, all alone,
Alone on a wide wide sea!

> And never a saint to pity on
> My soul in agony.[1]

Finally, there is the loneliness of responsibility. In the novel *Moby Dick,* by Herman Melville, the preacher climbs a rope ladder to a high pedestal. Once there, he pulls the ladder up behind him before he delivers his message to the shipmates. This is the loneliness of responsibility. It is going by yourself to a restricted area in your line of duty. The shepherd experiences all these kinds of loneliness. He sees all of the colors in this kaleidoscope of loneliness. Furthermore, in the past there were no united shepherding organizations. The sheep could not understand why the shepherd would weep when a lamb was lost or rejoice when it was found. The primary relationship of the shepherd is not with other human beings but with sheep.

Third, shepherding is a love-expressing work. It is a vocation of tender affection; that is, the true shepherd is one who works for the sake of his work in the platonic sense, not the man who works only for profit, whom Jesus calls "a hireling." All artists have portrayed the shepherd as protecting, feeding, tending, leading his sheep, and risking his life to save one of the fold. With winds sweeping the atmosphere, lightning sticking its flaming finger through the black clouds, with rolling thunder preceding the chill of a coming storm, we see the faithful shepherd on the mountainside, feeling his way in the night through thickets and briar patches, listening for the low bleating of one lost lamb.

Jesus became transparent before this portrait. He picked up the title of shepherd and wore it as a well-fitting garment. He made it luminous without rending its tissue. He took it with him through the gates of glory without emptying it of its sweet human significance. "I am," said he, "the good shepherd."

His was a lowly estate. His was so lowly that he was born in a village barn. His was so lowly that he wore a seamless garment by day and slept in it by night, so lowly that he put his lips to the bucket after having begged for a drink at a public well by the roadside. His was a lonely work. Long before his footfalls were heard in Nazareth, Isaiah carved a prophetic path for him to tread. In Jesus' supreme moments of trial, he was by himself. See him, alone in Gethsemane's hanging garden. See him, a man of sorrows and acquainted with grief, stretched out on Calvary's crossbeam, crying, "My God, my God, why hast thou forsaken me?" His was a love-expressing work. His

[1] *The Rime of the Ancient Mariner,* part 4, lines 232-235.

was a love that, like the roots of a rosebush, went down into the crude earth and drew glorious colors and ravishing perfume out of the soil. It was a love that emptied itself to feed others, a love that threw itself between the wolf and the sheep.

II. An inclusive concern

The contemporaries of Christ were inclined to religious exclusiveness, feeling that they were the only people in God's pasture, the only sheep of his hand, like the German Nazis, believing themselves the Herrenvolk, and the World War II Japanese, who considered themselves the sons of heaven. Jewish contemporaries of Jesus considered themselves superior people, saved by God's partiality for a privileged salvation. Jesus startled them when he said, "Other sheep have I which are not of this fold." Christ put the seal of preciousness on every human being.

This is instructive for us today. It teaches that there is one Lord, one faith, one baptism, one Shepherd, and one flock which is inclusive of all humanity.

The problem lies in our misunderstanding of the fact that some persons are outside of the fold of the blessed. They are still sheep, inside or outside of the fold, but in the latter category they are simply lost. We need not go to remote areas of Australia or to the jungles of Asia or cities of Africa or the hinterlands of South America to find them. Any stroll down the main streets of our own cities or towns, any walk in our neighborhoods, any look at our extended and sometimes nuclear families will bring them into our view. We call them names outside the church. We call them exceptional children, offenders, addicts, pushers, pimps, prostitutes, derelicts, psychopaths, alcoholics, freaks, militants, hippies, and other so-called deviants. Inside the church we call them inactive members, backsliders, hypocrites, profit cultists, heretics, loose liberals, and die-hard conservatives; and we group all the rest under the title of "sinner." Many of us feel our consciences eased when we encounter a man with a problem; we put him in a category, giving the appropriate title to him, and move on. We say, "Look at that wino. What a shame!" Then we move on, unmindful that that man in the gutter is a bona fide member of the flock of God. The only difference between him and us is that he is lost. And if our attitudes don't change, we, like him, will be lost. He may be lost because of weakness, stubbornness, ignorance, or preoccupation, but he is lost. He may be, through shrewd calculation, like the prodigal son who sought to violate the law of love, to sip the pleasures of sin while the red blood was still dancing in his veins. He may be lost through carelessness of others or through the mischances of life, like the coin which escaped the woman's notice until it slipped through her fingers and seemed nowhere to be found, or he may be lost like the little lamb which blunderingly and foolishly wandered away from the fold and the shepherd. But it does not matter how a man became lost, dislocated, or misplaced; he still needs to be found. Jesus came to find such a person. "The Son of man is come to seek and to save that which was lost" (Luke 19:10, KJV). Like him who sends us we should associate with fallen fishermen, confused rulers, crooked tax collectors, misguided women, the unemployed, and the outcast and by the Spirit bring them to the circle of love which we know is the fold of the blessed.

III. A personal relevance

Jesus said, "I know my own [sheep] and my own [sheep] know me" (John 10:14). His knowledge is deep and intimate. In the Old Testament, when Isaac was led to the altar of sacrifice, the boy asked his father, Abraham, "Where is the lamb?" (Genesis 22:7). This question remained typologically unanswered for centuries. It loomed over Jacob's stone and David's harp and resounded over Solomon in all the glory of his crumbling kingdom. It soared over Elijah's cave and Ezekiel's valley and Jeremiah's fountain of tears. It sounded and resounded through the corridors of time until John the Baptist, the rugged forerunner standing in the placid waters of the Jordan River, said, "Behold the Lamb of God, which taketh away the sin of the world" (John 1:29, KJV). He is the Shepherd who humbled himself until he became as a sheep led to the slaughter and the Lamb slain from the foundation of the world. He knows each one of his sheep; he knows of you, Christian believer: the name that you have, the street that you live on, the place where you work, and that which is around you—your friends by your side, the dreams in your soul, the disappointments in your life, the aspirations in your heart, the possibilities in your destiny. "I am," said he, "the good shepherd." The Greek word translated "good" is *kalos;* it literally means beautiful. When the Swiss theologian Karl Barth was asked, "What is beautiful?" he said, "That which fulfills its function." We go to a football game, and our favorite star intercepts a pass and runs ninety yards through brutes of the opposite team for the winning touchdown, and we exclaim, "That's beautiful!" We go to the NIT [an annual basketball tournament], and our favorite basketball player, in the last seconds of the game with the score tied, shoots the ball and hits the nets for the winning basket, and we say, "That's beautiful!" A singer that we know and love performs, and her voice is marvelous, and she sings with style and grace, and we say, "That's beautiful!" Christ is the beautiful Shepherd; he has a shepherd's eyes and misses not one of the flock; he has a shepherd's heart, beating with pure and generous love; he has a shepherd's strength so that he will be able to defend us; he has a shepherd's gentleness and carries the young lamb in the bosom of his care. A personal, beautiful Shepherd!

There is an old story about a church that gave a scholarship to one of its young members to attend a college some distance away. When the youth returned for his Christmas break during the first year, he visited the church as was his custom on Sunday evenings when he lived near there. With the desire to demonstrate the worthiness of the investment in him, he decided to demonstrate something of what he had learned. At the conclusion of the meeting, when he was recognized, he asked the director to permit him a moment to recite Psalm 23. The director was pleased, and the people gladly watched him as he strode with youthful steps to the podium of the auditorium. He did a splendid job reciting the psalm. His clear, resonant voice indicated a mastery of diction and inflection as he crossed every elocutional *t* and dotted every *i*. When he finished, there was a spontaneous burst of applause and cheers. But in the back of the room there was an elderly lady who, inspired by the young man's delivery, raised her hand to ask permission to say a word to the gathering. Though the hour was late and the people restless, the director gave his hesitant consent. Slowly, the aged woman made her way down the aisle, leaning on each pew she passed, for the snow of the winter had gathered in her hair, and her back was bent under the weight of the decades. When she got to the podium, she was out of breath and leaned on the lectern. She said softly the words of that same psalm. Her voice was weak, and her diction was poor; her formal education had ended with grammar school, and her pronunciation and enunciation left much to be desired; but when she had finished, mothers clasped their children, and fathers who had long been strangers to tears found new fountains. The spirits of the people were moved as the rushing wind moves the trees of the wood.

Later, someone asked the director, "What was the difference between the two speakers? Why was it that when the college student spoke, the people cheered, but when the woman spoke, people wept?" The director, with a light in his eye, said, "I know the difference. The student knew the psalm, but the saint knew the Shepherd." Do you know the Shepherd? Can you say, "The Lord is my Shepherd"?

O. C. Jones, Jr., is an Area Representative for the Ministers and Missionaries Benefit Board of the American Baptist Churches in the U.S.A. and works out of the Los Angeles area. He is a member of the Trinity Baptist Church in Los Angeles, where he serves as assistant to the pastor in the capacity of Minister of Community Affairs. Previous to holding this position, he was the pastor of the Greater Mount Olive Baptist Church of Los Angeles and the Saint John Missionary Baptist Church of Long Beach, California. A native of Texas, he received degrees from the Pacific Christian College, Long Beach; California Baptist College and Theological Seminary (now American Baptist Seminary of the West at Covina, California); and the American Evangelical School of Divinity. He is currently a candidate for a Ph.D. from the California Graduate School of Theology at Glendale, California. He has had a wide range of experience in varied kinds of Christian service: a director of Christian education, evangelist, teacher, writer, and lecturer.

The Preacher's Dilemma

O. C. Jones, Jr.

> Sometimes I think God has put us apostles at the very end of the line,
> like prisoners soon to be killed, put on display at the end of a victor's
> parade, to be stared at by men and angels alike (1 Corinthians 4:9, *The
> Living Bible*).

Several months after A. C. Craig was ordained to the gospel
ministry, principal Alexander Martin met him on Prince Street in
Edinburgh and greeted him with the question, "Well, how's the
preaching going?" When Craig replied that he was "finding it
difficult," Martin exclaimed, "Preaching's not difficult, man; it's
impossible!" This was, I am sure, a forcible epigram, spoken before
Reinhold Niebuhr had accustomed a generation of theological
students to speak with easy familiarity about "impossible possibilities."

"Preaching's not difficult; it's impossible!" Let no man imagine
that he will ever master the glamorous, elusive art of preaching. If
you have an authentic call to it, it will enslave you, enchant you, tease
you, confound you all your days; and in the end you will still have to
say, "I have not attained; I only press toward the mark of this high
calling." The preacher must not be overcome by the horizontal
problems and difficulties which attend his calling. From these
problems and difficulties there can only be a partial and painful
measure of extrication, like that of a man struggling through a thicket
of briars who, before he gets free from one tangle of thorns, is
clutched by another. The Christian pulpit stands not only in a
mundane dimension of reality but also in the supernatural plane of
faith; and the man who speaks from it is charged to speak not only
about God but from God, not only as a reporter but also as an
ambassador. To see preaching in its true perspective is to be reminded
that every listener's ear ought to be turned to catch not merely a man's
words but God's Word through them. Ministerial responsibility is
enough to cause, as Barth calls it, "fundamental alarm." To the end of
time, preaching can only be an embarrassed stammering.

What Constitutes the Preacher's Dilemma?

The most exacting responsibility of the preacher is preaching as the regular diet of the church's worship to which the invitation is as wide as humanity itself. The preacher must preach past ignorance, prejudice, suspicion, and fear. The difficulty is aggravated since the audience comprises people of all ages, classes, and degrees of mental and spiritual attainment. How are you to pitch your utterance for such heterogeneous hearing? Suppose all these problems are solved in one measure or another; the thorniest problem of all still remains: "Who are you, yourself, who ventures to stand in a pulpit?" Barth directs some soul-stirring and soul-searching questions to the preacher when he asks him what he is doing and on what grounds he takes on the role of mediator between heaven and earth. Preachers are brazen and presumptuous! One does not with impunity usurp the prerogatives of God! Because preaching is what it is, no coward can be a preacher!

The preacher is a channel. He stands in a kind of "no man's land." Kings and warriors have not been the real molders of history. The embarrassed, stammering preachers, designated by Sylvester Horne as the "great hearts of the Calling," have been the real molders of history. Gospel sermons outlast the pyramids, outweigh the cargoes of commerce, and cast in the shade the acts of parliaments.

The Modern Congregation Has No Theological Grasp of the Faith

During the past half century, doctrinal trumpets have been blowing with an uncertain sound. We have had an overdose of butterfly preaching (a perpetual fluttering from one flowery text to another). As yet, little has been done to counteract the theological looseness and lostness of our time. Theological lostness is a different thing from irreligion. Religion is one thing; its reflective formulation into a system of doctrine is another.

Theology is to religion what a cup with a handle is to the man who wants to drink from a deep river. With the best of his mind, the deepest of his spirit, the utmost of his labor, and the finest of his art, the preacher must proclaim the fundamentals of the faith! The preacher must flood the intellectual and spiritual darkness of men with the qualities of divine lucidity and understanding.

Ignorance of the Bible and Uncertainty Regarding Its Authority

The thoughtful layman is well aware that some profound change has taken place in the church's attitude toward Scripture but finds it difficult to grasp what the change is, how much it implies, and where it is likely to lead. For his grandfather the Bible was a book of answers to life's problems, authoritative and divinely certified; for the layman today it has become a book of problems, too many to which there appear to be no authoritative answers; it is not even ecclesiastically authoritative, let alone divinely so. Are the biblical narratives which are the carriers of the gospel what they purport to be and what his grandfather held them to be—reliable accounts of historical events? Are they admixed with symbolism, allegory, legend, myth, and whatnot? Do they belong to primitive and obsolete ways of thinking? Have they been affected by bias and wishful thinking, colored by childish fancies, corrupted by error? If so, how much? And who is to say how much? Questions like these are the stock and trade of theological institutions so that their denizens, even if they cannot answer them, become gradually immunized to their upsetting effects.

However, it is different with the layman. The upsetting questions reach him like the rumors that run about in wartime and that are not always dispelled by smooth, official communiqués. People who never had very strong religious constitutions succumb easily. Others of tougher spiritual fiber, reverencing the Bible and having staked their lives on the truth of its teaching, are yet profoundly uneasy about the source of its authority. They are like polar explorers who wake up one morning to discover that their camp, instead of being pitched on the mainland, is adrift on an ice floe. Misgivings regarding the authority of the Bible are far from being automatically relieved by wider education and culture, except where the appropriate apologetic is being deliberately and vigilantly introduced. The reason is not hard to see; the wider education and culture of our day is predominantly scientific, not only in content but also in temper and predisposition. Modern science has drawn upon the traditional view of the Bible and necessitated some kind of reinterpretation of it. Until such a reinterpretation is as pervasive as science itself, the progress of education can only add to the confusion regarding the Bible.

And this leads me to say that whatever else our generation believes or disbelieves, it believes in science. The presuppositions of science have ousted all other premises and have become for many the master light of all their seeing. Some of these persons are Communists who envision, as one ex-Communist has put it, "the vision of man's mind displacing God as the creative intelligence of the world." Others who do not ally their scientific faith either with Marxist theory or

Communist practice hold their faith in divorce from any kind of theism. The working creed of such people runs something like this: Scientific thinking, bearing fruit in an all-pervading scientific attitude, promises to supply the resources by which man's economic standard of living can be raised and all his capacities for good living can be developed. It is possible, according to this scientific faith, to organize life in a national way so as to eradicate the international frictions leading to war and economic conflict; it is possible to produce and distribute man's worldly goods fairly and sensibly. According to this view, for the first time in history, man could have the opportunity and the incentive to break free from the petty squabbles and sordid "necessities" which act today as a powerful brake on his development. Provided that men could be cured of stupidity, human nature—the world itself—would slowly reach perfection here in history. And the cure for stupidity is education in the scientific attitude.

Now, thousands of our contemporaries—being neither Communists nor fellow travelers, but holding the scientific attitude—are no longer in the church. But remember that the people who are left in the pews are also profoundly affected by the buoyant and expanding scientific culture of our day. What do we Christians stand to gain or lose in this contemporary cultural crisis? What ought we to learn and unlearn? Against whom ought we to be fighting? With whom ought we to be seeking alliance and on what terms?

Some may think that all the church needs to do in our day is to put its house in order theologically, frame its faith anew, and set about indoctrinating its members in this postreformation model. It would doubtless be grand if we could forthwith unloose three hundred fiery-tailed theological foxes among the Philistine corn; but how to catch the cohort of foxes and to get fire affixed to their tails is the initial program.

The preacher must stand up and declare the Bible a strangely reverberating book, a book which has power to turn the tables on critical thinking. Up to a point the Bible submits to our judgment; then quick as a flash of lightning the roles are reversed, and the Bible starts to pronounce judgment upon us. The preacher must lead the church to demonstrate that revelation does not cease to be revelation when it is conveyed in earthen vessels, that science need not be repudiated in order to retain faith, nor faith be repudiated in order to vindicate the scientific method. The preacher must alert the master of arts to the possibility that bachelors of science might also be God's children.

The pulpit has one grand aim—to make Christ credible to a confused generation by reinstating the Book which testifies of Christ. Christ disturbs! The devil's favorite Sunday morning entertainment is the sermon which does not disturb. The pulpit must have something relevant, serious, and honest to say on perplexing problems and subjects. To remain silent on difficult subjects is an embarrassed evasion of duty rather than the solution of a problem. The miraculous element is found in both the Old and New Testaments. The miraculous is a valid concept which must not be thrown to the scientists as though the church was fleeing for its life. Miracle is a valid concept because infinite love armed with infinite power can stretch down from heaven to earth to avert disaster and confer salvation. An inrush of omnipotence shatters the test tubes of science. Infinite love armed with infinite power can transcend the laws by which a thing *can't* be done and discover a higher law by which it *can* be done. "The Lord's hand is not shortened, that it cannot save; neither his ear heavy, that it cannot hear" (Isaiah 59:1, KJV). Every miracle story in the Bible has as its ultimate theme the power of God who reveals himself as the righteous Redeemer, a very present help in time of trouble to those who put their trust in him.

What constitutes the authority of the Bible? Wherein lies its authority? The authority of the Bible derives solely and entirely from its intrinsic power to make men aware of God as a reality. The Bible's intrinsic power is constant. Nothing that the church can say can add in the slightest way to it; and nothing that philosophers or scientists can say, no dogma based on extrabiblical presupposition, can subtract in the slightest way from it. The God whom we confront in the Bible is a miracle-working God. It is in his nature to do wondrous things in mercy and judgment.

The God of the Bible is the Creator. Creativity is often used in a diluted sense of artistic originality, but in the Bible creation is the divine prerogative, the exercise of which excites awe rather than admiration. One sees this in the sublimity of passages like the fortieth chapter of Isaiah or the thirty-eighth chapter of Job, in which the writers contemplate the mysterious hinterland of absolute creative energy which lies behind the majestic coastline of nature. The God of the Bible is the Creator. He fixed the infinitesimally small speck of dust. He fixed a bewilderingly exhaustless profusion of suns and systems and constellations and nebulae which staggers the mind. Besides creating our own little solar system, God created countless other suns and systems far more illustrious than ours—blazing superstars beyond estimation, around which swing myriads of globes with their belts and rings and treasures; immeasurable thoroughfares of glory; ocean after ocean of constellations; colossal stars which could absorb our own sun and planets without adding one beam to their splendor or a sprinkling of dust to their magnitude; burning stars which are only kept from destroying us because of the immense expanses intervening; groups of stars amassed like gigantic stellar cities; choirs of worlds; and crowded congregations of celestial marvels. Were it possible to run the gamut of all these, there still would be no sign of the universe's border or of the hem on creation's garment of space!

Let the preacher stand up and declare the God of the Bible, the God revealed in Jesus Christ. There is a systematic and determined effort on the part of some people to discredit preachers and preaching. But such will not succeed. Why?—because the idea behind preachers and preaching is divine.

Preachers and Preaching Are Divine

> Then the word of the Lord came unto me, saying, Before I formed thee in the belly I knew thee; and before thou camest forth out of the womb I sanctified thee, and I ordained thee a prophet unto the nations. Then said I, Ah, Lord God! behold, I cannot speak: for I am a child. But the Lord said unto me, Say not, I am a child: for thou shalt go to all that I shall send thee, and whatsoever I command thee thou shalt speak. Be not afraid of their faces: for I am with thee to deliver thee, saith the Lord. Then the Lord put forth his hand, and touched my mouth. And the Lord said unto me, Behold, I have put my words in thy mouth (Jeremiah 1:4-9, KJV).

In a daring sweep of prophecy the apostle Paul hailed the preacher as God's agent for the saving of mankind:

> For seeing that . . . the world through its wisdom knew not God, it was God's good pleasure through the foolishness of the preaching to save them that believe (1 Corinthians 1:21, American Standard Version).

Charlatans in the ministry and grafters in politics are barnacles; they did not build the ship. Preaching is rooted in the fact that our race has always been haunted by the sense of another—another spelled with a capital *A,* from whom primitive tribes fled as from an Arch-Fear; another to whom Jesus prayed as to the Great

Companion. Preaching is rooted in the awareness of Another. Preaching is rooted in the persuasive faith and piercing conviction that in Christ that Other has made known his love and will for mankind. Preaching is rooted in a mystery encompassing this shadowy show of earth. Our race has always understood the mood of the African chief who when asked about his belief in God replied, "We know at nighttime somebody goes among the trees, but we never speak of it." Somebody goes among the trees. Somebody flames in the dawn. Somebody stirs in the tremor of springtime. Somebody lifts a challenge in our conscience, like a banner unfurled. Somebody gleams through our compassion. Somebody goes by in the scientist's quest for truth. Somebody goes by in the artist's vision of beauty. Somebody prepares a table before us in the presence of the enemy. Somebody scatters the darkness of our night. Somebody dries our tears in the day of bitter sorrow. Somebody fashioned the host of heaven. Somebody gave the atom the structure that entrances the mathmatician. Somebody changes fading hopes into tapestries of fadeless glory. Somebody pencils mingled hues of glory upon every black storm cloud. Somebody shines the light of brilliant constellations upon dark nights of despair. Somebody calms the raging storm. Somebody knows all about our struggles, and he will guide "til the day is done." Somebody soothes more griefs than all the philosophy of the world. Somebody comforts the noble host of the poor in spirit. Somebody sings courage to the army of the disappointed. Somebody pours healing balm into the hearts of the disconsolate.

Finally, in spite of the concerted effort of arch critics, preachers and preaching will persist. The preacher's call was not thundered from the sky nor written in letters of fire across the night; it came with a greater compulsion! Preaching is rooted in our seeking for God and in his prior seeking for us.

Churches change, but the prophet abides. The sky opens to let him through. Group discussion and dialogue have a useful place, but they break in on history's logic if either tries to silence the preacher's voice or the poet's song. The eternities have always chosen their own man— some, Isaiah from his princely home; some, Abraham from his land of Chaldean idolatry; some, youthful and sensitive Jeremiah; some, trumpet-throated John the Baptist; some, Amos from the plow—and his word has not been the group's word. There is in the preacher's soul an inevitable swing of the Spirit's tides, oncoming as of starry hosts; he must speak his word. But his office can never be his throne; rather, it is his altar where his life is laid down. Nor can it ever be arrogance; it is the conviction of his sin. It is his burden, his doom, and his exceeding joy. "Woe is me! . . . for mine eyes have seen the King . . ." (Isaiah 6:5, KJV). Yet, in his great unworthiness, he must tell what he has seen. For "woe is unto me, if I preach not the gospel!" (1 Corinthians 9:16, KJV).

One of the critics' sharper thrusts is that the preacher doesn't do anything but pour out words. How true! But let it be remembered: words are deeds. The Greeks said, "By words alone are lives of mortals swayed." Another voice, more quiet and searching (the Word made flesh), said to us, "Heaven and earth shall pass away, but my words shall not pass away" (Matthew 24:35, KJV). Words are tools. Speech is an agency. Words born in the soul's silence are among earth's mightiest tools. Words—a brush to paint pictures, a chisel to carve motives, a battering ram to break down the walls of oppression, a compass to guide the traveler, a light to pierce the soul's gloom. Such is "The Preacher's Dilemma," in which is also found his greatest joy.

James V. Matthews is pastor of St. Benedict's Church in Oakland, California. Among other responsibilities he is a member of the Board of Directors of the National Black Catholic Clergy Caucus; executive secretary of the Bay Area Black Catholic Caucus; a member of the Oakland Diocese Pre-Seminary Board of Directors; and a Knight of St. Peter Claver, a black Catholic religious and fraternal organization. He was born and raised in California and received his B.A. degree in humanities/philosophy from St. Patrick's College in Mountain View, California, and his Master of Divinity degree from St. Patrick's Seminary in Menlo Park, California.

When, from Our Exile . . .

James V. Matthews

Several years ago, black priests and black laymen and laywomen were telling me and other black Catholics in this country that *hope* for the Catholic church in the black community rests mainly on black Catholics who must shoulder the responsibility of affecting changes that will breathe new life into the Catholic church, especially the church in the black community.

Looking around me at black Catholics that I grew up with and met during my early seminary days, I became very discouraged and disheartened, for *we* definitely were not ready to begin the necessary changes that would have breathed new life into Catholicism in our diocese—*so I thought!*

I saw around me a fragmented, alienated, disunified group of black Catholics:

(*a*) Black Catholics who were proud to be Catholics and great defenders of the faith but were not very proud of the fact of being called black.

(*b*) Some black Catholics who wanted very much to make Catholicism relevant to the black community but would be in danger of giving up, sacrificing their Catholic heritage in order to be relevant.

(*c*) Other black Catholics who were trying to come to grips with both a positive black identity and their Catholic heritage but were too "heavy" for the bishop and their pastors.

My discouragement and skepticism about black Catholics shouldering the responsibility of breathing new life and changes into the church was heightened by this fragmentation among the black Catholics I knew.

Looking back on the *history* of black people in this country, and especially the history of black Catholics in the church, our experience has always been that of *fragmentation, segregation,* and *disunity* among ourselves. Our experience as black people in the Catholic church has been one of *fringe-area participation;* we have rarely been allowed to participate in the mainstream of Catholicism. Our experience as Catholics in this country was similar to the experience of the Israelites, spoken of by the prophet Ezekiel, an experience of being ravaged and seized, plundered and made laughingstocks by their neighbors (Ezekiel 36:1-5).

But throughout our history of fringe-area participation and humiliation as black Catholics, we have survived as strong black Catholics who are true and faithful to our Catholic heritage without ceasing to be black. And *I believe* that the credit and responsibility for our survival should go to those black Catholics before us who paved the way for our survival from humiliation and token participation in the church.

These black men and women took their faith in Jesus seriously and tried as deeply as possible to *live out* the gospel. These men and women were truly *reborn* through water and the Spirit (see John 3:3-8), so much so that they were able to breathe new life into the church by struggling to incorporate black Catholics into the mainstream of Catholicism.

During the middle of the nineteenth century, these pioneering men and women began to emerge as full members in the Catholic church in America. In his quiet manner and strong determination James Augustine Healy overcame all sorts of prejudice and discrimination to become a priest and to serve in the United States. Because of his faith and strong will, he succeeded, against all odds, in being ordained. Father Healy was a very successful priest and pastor in Boston and eventually became the first black bishop in this country. He paved the way for his two brothers to become priests, as well as for his many other black brothers who became priests serving in the continental United States.

Black women had religious vocations as well. But their struggle to materialize their vocations was much more difficult than that of men. Young men during these times were able to study for the priesthood outside the United States; but they had no guarantee that they would be able to return home after ordination. With young black women this was not the case. *No* religious community would accept black women. Therefore, with determination and filled with extraordinary faith, these women set out to establish their own religious communities: the Oblate Sisters of Providence, Baltimore, Maryland; the Blessed Sacrament Sisters of Baltimore, Maryland; and the Holy Family Sisters of New Orleans, Louisiana.

There was a small group of black laymen and laywomen who wanted very much to become part of the mainstream of Catholicism. Because of their faith and efforts, the Knights and Ladies of Peter Claver were established in order to participate collectively in parish life; to promote civic participation; to encourage and carry out

Catholic, apostolic, and social action; to develop youth; and to provide social and religious fellowship among Christians.

These pioneer black Catholics, *our unsung heroes* who definitely were born of the Spirit, heard the *call* of faith and unity and were not afraid to take *risks* for the sake of unity.

Today, we must be reborn in the Spirit; we must open our eyes, our hearts, and our ears to hear the *call* for unity. We must throw off the yokes of fragmentation, alienation, and disunity. Because of our rebirth through water and the Spirit, we are assured that God has given each of us a new heart and a new spirit. As black Catholics, we must not be disheartened and discouraged over our past fragmentation and disunity. Hopefully, we will overcome them.

We have the responsibility to continue the struggle to emerge as true and authentic black Catholics without ceasing to be black.

We must be willing to deal with and live with one another as brothers and sisters in the Lord, rather than being concerned with *pettiness* and *needlessly* becoming suspicious of the motives and abilities of our brothers and sisters.

We must always be willing to come together to celebrate our call to unity as brothers and sisters in Christ, who have the faith and the strength to affirm positively ourselves as black and Catholic and to affirm our history and our destiny in faith. We, definitely, are on our way. Amen.

Olin P. Moyd is the pastor of the Mount Lebanon Baptist Church in Baltimore, Maryland. He is also active in the American Baptist denomination, having served on the Executive Board of the American Baptist Churches of the South (ABCOTS) and as moderator of the Maryland Area ABCOTS. He serves as an advisor to the National Black Catholic Caucus and has served as the leader of several local and national Christian education institutes. He lectures on the black experience before various local and national groups and has published several articles on the subject of the black religious experience. A native of South Carolina, he is a graduate of the Cortez W. Peters Business School. He also received degrees from Temple Theological College, New York, New York; Morgan State College, Baltimore, Maryland; and Howard University School of Religion, Washington, D.C. He also received honorary degrees from Temple Theological College and Virginia Seminary and College, Lynchburg, Virginia.

Membership or Movement?

Olin P. Moyd

Luke 9:57-62

Setting Out

There is in our tradition a song which goes as follows:

> I'm on my way
> to the kingdom land,
> I'm on my way
> to the kingdom land,
> I'm on my way
> to the kingdom land,
> I'm on my way,
> Oh, Lord, I'm on my way.
> If you don't go,
> I'll journey on,
> If you don't go,
> I'll journey on,
> If you don't go,
> I'll journey on,
> I'm on my way,
> Oh, Lord, I'm on my way.

It is clear that the creators and faithful participants in the singing of this song saw themselves involved in a movement. The lack of involvement on the part of others would neither dampen their spirits nor hamper their journey. But this is not a new phenomenon. It evolved with the patriarchs and prophets of old, and it was endorsed by Jesus of Nazareth.

This brings us to a line from a verse preceding our primary text: "And it came to pass, when the time was come that he should be received up, he steadfastly set his face to go to Jerusalem" (Luke 9:51, KJV).

Jesus had reached an irreversible decision to go to Jerusalem, and nothing was to deter him. As in every movement, some side issues did arise: again from the preceding verses, Jesus sent some unnamed messengers to an unnamed village of the Samaritans. Here, neither the names of the messengers nor the name of the village is important. These are side issues. They might have been important for sociological studies, but they were only peripheral to salvation. The fact that Jesus had a steadfast focus on Jerusalem is clearly stated. Periodically, Christians became so bogged down in side issues that their focus upon the primary Christian objective often became diluted and distorted.

So Luke does not weary us at this point with names of messengers and villages. This treaty is more theological in implication than it is historical in explication. Having been denied and refused goods and services by the villagers, some of the disciples felt that this was a terrible and threatening tragedy to their physical well-being as well as that of their Lord and Master. So they hastily advanced this idea: "Lord, those who have not cooperated ought to be eliminated; do you want us to command fire to come down from heaven and consume them, as Elias did?" (see Luke 9:54.) But the divinity of Jesus immediately detected the fact that his disciples were about to be trapped into the temptations of side issues. He was not going to let the physical needs of the disciples become a stumbling block to their heavenly purpose. And he was not going to let the earthly weaknesses of the disciples stand in the way of the heavenly will of the Father. Thus, Jesus broke in with a declarative statement: ". . . the Son of man is not come to destroy men's lives, but to save them . . ." (Luke 9:56, KJV). This statement must have been so deep and direct that there was no need for further dialogue on the matter. All that Luke tells us is that at this point, they went to another village. Here is an eternal movement on its way to fulfillment, shifting from scene to scene.

The Applicants for Membership

The truth which Jesus proclaimed and the righteousness which he exhibited transcended the boundaries of his physical travels. And truth has an irresistible, magnetic pull. Righteousness has a persuasive eloquence. Everybody wants to be on the side of truth. Everybody wants to be identified with righteousness. In other words, show me a church where there is a reputation of truth and righteousness, and I will show you a church where there are streams of applicants for membership.

Jesus had just arrived in this new village, and someone rushed up to him with his membership application. To bring that ancient dialogue into today's vernacular, the applicant said, "Lord, I have heard all about your mighty works; I have heard about your moving wonders; I have heard about your fearless faith; and I had hoped that you would one day come this way, because I wanted to join your group. Now, I will follow you wherever you go." Jesus raised the question: "Do you want merely to join this membership, or is it your intention to become involved in this movement?" "Just what do you mean, Lord?" "Well," said Jesus, "many folks have joined this membership since we started out, but when the ways got rough and the goings got tough, they fainted and faded. Although they had joined the membership, they had never committed themselves to become involved in this movement."

Jesus then offered a rhythmic explanation of one aspect of the movement:

> "Foxes have holes,
>   and birds of the air have nests;
>   but the Son of man hath
>   not where to lay his head" (Luke 9:58, KJV).

We can only speculate as to what response came from this first applicant. Another man was invited to become a part of the movement. But he begged to be excused to go first and bury his father. On the surface this appears to be a legitimate excuse to the logical and practical mind. But Jesus' quick response had the tone of being illogical and impractical. He initiates a new order of undertakers. ". . . Let the dead bury their dead: but go thou and preach the kingdom of God" (Luke 9:60, KJV). The fact of the matter is that this statement of our Master was neither illogical nor impractical. At this point the divinity of Jesus had detected the insincerity of the applicant. He wanted membership in the organization; he wanted his name on the roll; but he had no intentions of taking those risks which were an inevitable aspect of the movement. Thus, this statement of Jesus had little to do with the lack of respect or lack of sympathy for the man who had lost a father. It had to do with the lack of readiness for service and involvement in the movement on the part of this young man.

The excuse of the third applicant was that of needing time to bid farewell to his house guests. It is a further illustration of a confrontation between divinity (Jesus) and insincerity (the applicant).

At another point in time, a young man came to Jesus. His mission was that of ascertaining the means by which one could inherit eternal life. After a dialogue which showed that the young man was both acquainted with and an ardent keeper of the commandments, Jesus,

59

still detecting a deficiency in his spiritual character, said: ". . . go and sell that thou hast, and give to the poor, and thou shalt have treasure in heaven: and come and follow me" (Matthew 19:21, KJV). This the man was not committed to do. He was not ready for a movement that required this kind of involvement.

I need to inject here that in this encounter Jesus was not against the possession of money. Jesus realized that money was needed in the market. But money was not the basic necessity in this movement. Jesus could envision this fellow's intentions of using his money to pay his way through the impending difficulties of the movement. He might have attempted to use money in the place of mercy at some future point. For example, the situation in Gethsemane called for *praying* and not for *paying;* there was no provision for *paying* one's way out of Gethsemane. We must learn from this lesson. Money is *needful* today, but it is not all that is *needed* in the Christian movement.

Last year I attended the National Baptist Convention in Buffalo, New York. Our travel agent had made provisions for all of our transportation. Upon arrival at the airport, we were soon met by a gentleman who identified himself as the driver of our chartered bus which was to transport us to our hotel in Niagara Falls, Canada. While we were loading the bus, two delegates to the Convention who had come from another part of the country and who were not members of our party approached us; they were going to the same hotel as we were, and they had made no prearrangements to get from the airport to Canada. So they wanted to go on our bus; they assured us that they had money and were willing to pay the charges. However, the problem was not whether or not they had sufficient money to pay their way; the problem was whether or not we had available seats on the bus. Allow me to state this crudely: the solution to the situation depended not upon the *money* of the applicants but upon the *mercy* of those in our movement. We were able to provide seats for the applicants. They then joined our membership and paid their fare, but this was just a peripheral association. As soon as the crisis situation was over, upon arriving at the hotel, the two who had joined our membership faded into the larger throng of delegates.

It is one thing to join the Christian membership. It is something else to become involved in the Christian movement. The Christian churches today are not looking for joiners. We have plenty of them. In the face of irresistible truth and in the presence of the persuasive eloquence of right and righteousness, people join the membership, some of whom we have not seen since they joined.

Jesus of Nazareth, whose face was set steadfastly toward Jerusalem, who confronted the insincerity of those applicants in ancient times, this same Jesus is our Christ of faith; and he confronts our generation day by day. The challenge is not one of increasing membership; it is rather a challenge of involvement in a movement. We are moving from scene to scene. We are moving from plateau to plateau. We are moving, I tell you, moving from earth to glory.

Our faces are set steadfastly toward the new Jerusalem. In this movement there is no personal guarantee. In this movement there is no personal security. In this movement there is no personal honor. In this movement one runs the risk of being rejected. But let us not permit the hope on the horizon to become distorted while we look back, groping and groaning over the darkness and despairs around and behind us.

Jesus' final warning to the last applicant in the text was: ". . . No man, having put his hand to the plough, and looking back, is fit for the kingdom of God" (Luke 9:62, KJV). In this movement one must assume the posture of an experienced plowman. He never looks back. His eyes are steadfastly set upon the goal ahead.

While there are no temporal guarantees in this movement, there is an eternal assurance for those whose association goes deeper than mere membership. For those who are totally involved in this movement, there is the assurance of the eternal presence of the invisible hand of the Almighty.

His invisible hand
    pulls down the hills of oppression.
His invisible hand
    elevates the valleys of the disinherited.
His invisible hand
    is leveling the rough places before weary pilgrims.

The invisible hand of the Almighty sustains those of us in this movement. And from time to time we join the hymnologist Isaac Watts:

> O God, our help in ages past,
> Our hope for years to come,
> Our shelter from the stormy blast,
> And our eternal home,—
> And our eternal home,—

61

Beneath the shadow of Thy throne
Thy saints have dwelt secure;
Sufficient is Thine arm alone,
And our defense is sure,
And our defense is sure.

Eternity, with all its years,
Stands present in Thy view;
To Thee there's nothing old appears;
Great God, there's nothing new,
Great God, there's nothing new.

Our lives thro' various scenes are drawn,
And vexed with trifling cares,
While Thine eternal tho't moves on
Thine undisturbed affairs,
Thine undisturbed affairs.

William J. Shaw is the pastor of the White Rock Baptist Church in Philadelphia, Pennsylvania. Born in Marshall, Texas, he received his Bachelor of Arts degree from Bishop College, Dallas, Texas, and his Bachelor of Divinity degree from Union Theological Seminary. He was also awarded the Doctor of Ministry degree by Colgate Rochester Divinity School/Bexley Hall/Crozer. He has traveled widely and has studied in the University of Lagos, Lagos, Nigeria, West Africa; and the University of Ghana, Legon, Ghana, West Africa. Among his many responsibilities, he is chairman of the Executive Board of the Pennsylvania State Baptist Convention; a member of the Board and treasurer of OICs of America, Inc.; a member of the Board of Directors of Union Theological Seminary; and a member of the Board of Trustees of Bishop College.

A Day of Trouble

William J. Shaw

And it came to pass, when king Hezekiah heard it, that he rent his clothes, and covered himself with sackcloth, and went into the house of the Lord. And he sent . . . to Isaiah the prophet the son of Amoz. And they said unto him, Thus saith Hezekiah, This day is a day of trouble, and of rebuke, and blasphemy: for the children are come to the birth, and there is not strength to bring forth . . . wherefore lift up thy prayer for the remnant that are left (2 Kings 19:1-4, KJV).

Hezekiah's reign had begun with such great promise. He had initiated efforts designed to effect purity within the practice of religion and integrity within the political process. He removed the high places, broke the images, cut down the groves, and broke into pieces the brazen serpent which had become the occasion for idolatry within Judah. Trusting in the Lord God of Israel, he had thrown off the yoke of vassalage to the mighty Assyrian Empire and had striven successfully against the Philistines to secure the territorial borders of his tiny country.

Slowly but surely, the ideals of the leader began to infect and grasp the imaginations of the led. It did not happen overnight. Acts of revolution may occur, but the transformation of the souls of the revolters and the substantive implementation of the goals of reform often proceed at a much slower pace. Dreams may be dreamed in a night which may require the length of a lifetime to come to pass. Even so, with persistence dreams can come true, plans can issue into productivity. So, here and there, and then nearly everywhere, one could sense the rise of a new spirit in Judah. A new awareness of belonging was brooding beneath the surface. It appeared that they could really become what the king had purposed and God had intended.

But alas! After fourteen years of growing, a foe which had lurked menacingly on the horizons for all that time reared itself full length and dared to challenge all that Judah had been about. Emissaries from Sennacherib, king of Assyria, came bearing threats and taunts:

. . . Let not Hezekiah deceive you: for he shall not be able to deliver you . . . Neither let Hezekiah make you trust in the Lord, saying, The Lord will surely deliver us. . . . Hath any of the gods of the nations delivered at all his land out of the hand of the king of Assyria? (2 Kings 18:29-33, KJV).

65

The threats and taunts hit with unnerving impact because they were buttressed by the knowledge that they were historically accurate. No nation, no people, no matter their god, had been able to withstand Assyria till now. What's more, Judah had the memory of the fall of its sister people to the North some eight years prior. The Northern Kingdom had worshiped Jehovah and had fallen. What reason was there to believe that the Southern Kingdom, Judah, would have better fare?

An eerie silence settled over the land, for the king had commanded the people that they were not to answer Sennacherib. Watching, waiting, they looked then to Hezekiah for a word. He did not rush to speak, for his counsel now to the nation must be wise and saving. How did he weigh the situation? What were the prospects? What actions would he take? While servants watched, without a word Hezekiah rent his clothes, covered himself with sackcloth, and went into the house of the Lord. There he beckoned to his servants and broke his silence with the command: "Go brief the prophet! Tell Isaiah, 'This day is a day of trouble and of rebuke and blasphemy; for the children are come to the birth, and there is not strength to bring forth.'"

This message is explosive. It bursts and resonates across the centuries. The echo of these words, the substance of this briefing breaks the neat boundaries by which time is categorized. It defies the containment of history past and confronts us as a description of contemporary life. The words of Hezekiah to Isaiah have become the Word of God to our generation. Hear it well.

"The children are come to the birth." Here is a description of time's fullness. Time is neither void nor still. It moves, and it incubates. It is the womb of development. It has appropriate and inappropriate moments. And it knows now a condition of fullness. All conditions have been met for new life, a new being, a new order to come forth.

It is to be noted that the description of the text refers to a time in the *nation's* life. It was the fullness of time—when Judah's resolve to be a people free for God and under God was to stand the test of actualization. Now is also the fullness of time—when the promises of the American Constitution are to become the full possession of all its citizens. Now is the fullness of time—when colonialized nations have resolved to throw off the yokes of political, economic, and cultural serfdom and become themselves free under God's sun. Now is the fullness of time—when the hour is religiously ripe for biblical righteousness, when human hearts are hungering for spiritual sustenance.

"The children are come to the birth." When, in the course of nature, time's fullness has come, then the next normal step is delivery. Such a moment creates an air of excited expectancy. The prospect of a "new thing" generates emotions of joy and glee. But alas! No joyful sounds are now heard. There are no auras of glee abounding. Instead of rejoicing, there is gloom hanging heavily, for though the children are come to the birth, "there is not strength to bring forth."

Delivery is expected, normal, and next—but not without strength. Power is needed to birth time's fullness. The mother needs strength to effect that final "push" through the birth canal. Such a push is delicate and dangerous. Power is needed because in birth there is pain in the process of passage. Not even the Son of God could escape this. Redemption's new life was not possible except by Calvary's pain. The sinner's new life is not possible except he knows the pain of confessed guilt. We often forget the pain factor in trying to usher in history's possibilities and are unprepared to experience the agonies of its birth process.

How sad! There is not strength to actualize. Our nation lacks the moral will, the spiritual fiber to become what the Constitution sets forth. How sad! There is not strength to bring forth; colonialized nations embraced political freedom only to find themselves still economically weak and wasted, exploited too long to stand independently. There is much pain. How sad! There is not strength to bring forth; the hour is ripe for righteousness, but the organized religious fellowships—the churches, cathedrals, and synagogues of the land—are not marked by their commitment to the rigors of discipleship. So sad! This is the moment of new life, but all too many among blacks who have worked and wished for the new day are not now possessed of sufficient strength to enter into new life. The enemy to our aspirations sometimes seems stronger than the sources of our inspiration, and we have wearied of striving. Too many have become imitators of our oppressors.

This day, which ought to be a day of gladness, is a day of trouble. How do you define trouble? Not necessarily as agitation, rioting, and restlessness. These events, these traumas may sometimes be the pangs of new birth, the midwives of new life. Nay! Trouble as Scripture calls it here is not these. It is a time of trouble, says the Word, when potential is unrealized, when the greater good that can be and ought to be does not come to be. It is trouble when men lack the inner character to keep commitment with causes which are noble and lofty.

Trouble is often difficult to discern because for some, what *is,* is good; and they have no desire to risk for a supposed better. Trouble then is not the absence of good but the failure to realize the highest good. Herein lies the fault of America's failure of will. America fails to obtain the highest good because for too many what *is,* is good to them; and they will not risk their discomforting for the comforting of another and of all.

Trouble might be bearable, however, and men could decide to tolerate it, were it not for the fact that trouble turns to tragedy. There is tragedy for that which and those who struggle and strain for *life* only to be denied it. What happens to a people when their hope dies? When their future is foreclosed? When they come to the verge of realization only to find rejection? Even more so—what happens to that carrier of new life who prevents its birth? Let all who deny life to others, let the nations who would turn back time's clock when it has come to the moment of fullness, let them understand that they not only commit murder upon the life that is seeking to be, but they also commit suicide themselves. It is perilous to carry unborn life whose time has come in the womb. The carrier is infected and dies also. Beware and be warned, ye nations who prevent life. In causing death—you, too, die.

This day is a day of trouble—and of *blasphemy.* Here is the ultimate fright. Sennacherib taunted Hezekiah, but he in so doing also offended God. It is blasphemy when that which God has ordained is dishonored, denied, and fought by men. Sennacherib, what makes you think you have the right to deny freedom to Judah? "We hold these truths to be self-evident, that all men are created equal, that they are endowed by their Creator with certain unalienable Rights, that among these are Life, Liberty and the pursuit of Happiness"—so states the Declaration of Independence (1776). America, from whence comes your right to subjugate economically other nations? White man, from whence comes your authority to deny freedom to black men? Know ye not that your offenses against the least are crimes against the Almighty? This day of freedom's taunting and denial has ultimate dimensions.

Trouble, tragedy, blasphemy. What shall we do? Speak to us, Hezekiah. Direct us, O Spirit divine. Show us and tell us. Now glimmers of light faintly show themselves.

Let those in power know that this day is sanctuary time. Let them seek it. Hezekiah garbed himself fittingly and went into the temple. Rulers and leaders must not feign omnipotence. There is health in acknowledging that even *you* need help. Now is the time to lead the nation to frequent that abode where awareness of the holy is heightened. It is sanctuary time. Seek the place where vision is clarified. It is sanctuary time. Seek the site where character is cleansed and resolve is rectified. It is sanctuary time, and let none be misled into thinking that the sanctuary is the site where the struggle is abandoned. Nay! It is the place where the soul is buttressed for battle. Black folk have known this through the long dark days of slavery. Let them not forget it now in the continuing struggle for freedom.

But this alone is not enough. The religionists of our day must seek and brief the prophet. Shebna the scribe and the elders of the priests, at Hezekiah's directions, carried word to the prophet. Our land needs to hear not the keepers of the houses of religion, but the guardians of the soul of religion—the prophets. Tell the prophet! Would that all preachers and pastors were prophets! Tell the prophet! He is concerned not merely with personal purity and private morality but with national policy as well. Tell the prophet! It is a concern of true religion when purpose is pawned for corporate profit. Tell the prophet, for the land is jeopardized when it comes to the brink of greatness and because of pain turns back. Tell the prophet! Get the ear of someone who has the ear of God! Tell him to pray. Tell him to talk to God. This has ofttimes proved to be the route to redemption.

Still one other course is suggested. Sennacherib persisted in his threats and reduced the same to writing, whereupon Hezekiah, having received the same, took the missive into the temple and spread it open upon the altar. There he prayed: ". . . Open, Lord, thine eyes, and see: and hear the words of Sennacherib . . ." (2 Kings 19:16, KJV).

This is the ultimate step, the highest act of religion and faith—when one is willing to lay his case open fully before the Lord without condition. It allows God's own judgment to be set forth and indicates a willingness to follow whatever course he might dictate. It implies a willingness to be still before him, to wait upon him, to be accepting of whatever comes from him—in the belief that whatever he does is right.

Well did our parents display this spirit when they sang:

> Leave it there, leave it there,
> Take your burden to the Lord and leave it there.

If you trust and never doubt,
He will surely bring you out,
Take your burden to the Lord and leave it there.[1]

The land would do well to heed this advice and follow the example of Hezekiah. We have less merit on our side than he, but we can lay our case open before God nonetheless, hiding nothing and open to whatever. Perhaps he will have mercy. It is in his nature to be compassionate towards the penitent.

[1]C. Albert Tindley, "Leave It There." Copyright by Hope Publishing Company. Used by Permission.

J. Alfred Smith, Sr., is the pastor of the Allen Temple Baptist Church in Oakland, California. He is also an adjunct professor at seminaries in the Oakland-San Francisco Bay area. Previously, he was a member of the staff of the Ministers and Missionaries Benifit Board of the American Baptist Churches in the U.S.A. He received his B.S. degree from Western Baptist College, Kansas City, Missouri; his B.D. and Th.M. degrees from Missouri School of Religion, Columbia, Missouri; his M.A. in church history from the American Baptist Seminary of the West, Berkeley, California; and his D.Min. degree from Golden Gate Baptist Theological Seminary. He has delivered many lectures and written many editorials as well as a number of books, including *Preach On!, The Overflowing Heart,* and *Deacons Upholding the Pastor's Arms.*

The Future of the Black Church

J. Alfred Smith, Sr.

Matthew 15:31-39

"You are what you are when you act."

—Simone Devereaux

"No matter how high you are, you are only as high as the lowest of your people."
—Calvin Hill, running back, Dallas Cowboys and student at Perkins
School of Theology

In America, there are almost sixteen million black Christians. Less than two million of the sixteen million are members of predominantly white denominations. Nonetheless, black congregations have a rich history. Persons who have been highly critical of the Afro-American Christian church are uninformed about the noble history of the church. In fact, the oldest of those institutions in the black community *is* the church.

Before our race had formal organizations to protest against the evil of slavery, the black church kept the flame of freedom burning in the hearts of our fathers. When slavery and oppression dehumanized our fathers, and when discrimination and segregation degraded them, the black church taught them to sing: "We are our heavenly Father's children. And we all know that he loves us, one and all."

When the fathers were weak physically and spiritually, when our mothers were robbed of hope, the words of the unlettered black preacher pushed them on with "Walk together, children; don't get weary!"

When death was nigh, our fathers in the ministry told the people that over yonder they would sit at the welcome table, eat and never get hungry, drink and never get thirsty.

From the womb of the black church came singers like Marian Anderson and Mahalia Jackson; educators like Mordecai Johnson and Benjamin Mays; politicians like Adam Clayton Powell, Jr., and Marshall Shepherd; civil rights leaders like Nat Turner and Martin Luther King, Jr.; preachers like D. A. Holmes and Gardner Taylor; community organizers like Jesse Jackson and Ralph Abernathy.

Time is too short and the list is too long for me to call more names. Can't we agree that the black church's past has been fruitful and productive?

The question, however, is with the future of the black church. Where is the church going? Will it enlarge upon its noble past? Will the acids of secularity deny the church of ebony hue a future pregnant with creative and constructive possibilities? What will Afro-American Christians do about working with God for the redemption and regeneration of society?

The black church cannot afford to face the future by being a weak imitation of a country club. The church building will have to serve not only the church membership *but also those persons of need in the community.* Jesus served people who were in need. The majority of the people he helped were of immoral character and low social standing.

The black church *must* strive to serve not only the classes but also the masses. Jesus served the masses. White Protestantism in America is primarily middle class-oriented. The black church cannot have middle class priorities. The black masses are not yet middle class. Let us reflect upon the sharp and stinging words of ex-preacher James Baldwin who said:

> White people cannot, in the generality, be taken as models of how to live. Rather, the white man is himself in sore need of new standards, which will release him from his confusion and place him once again in fruitful communion with the depths of his own being.[1]

You see, the white church has been silent on the great issues of racism, war, poverty, and injustice. White ministers who take stands on these issues find a backlash of declining budgets, smaller church attendance, and often letters telling them that they are terminated from their positions.

Simply to imitate white middle class churches with dignified worship and an educated clergy is not going far enough toward letting "justice run down as waters and righteousness as a mighty stream."

The black agenda calls for a church that will sponsor programs that will do the following:

1. encourage the youth with scholarship aid;
2. conduct programs that teach black youth dignity, pride, self-respect, accomplishment, and achievement;

[1]James Baldwin, *The Fire Next Time* (New York: The Dial Press, 1963), pp. 110-111.

3. conduct tutorial projects and remedial programs;
4. provide job and vocational counseling;
5. provide family life education and premarital counseling;
6. conduct black self-help and black economic development programs;
7. provide moral and spiritual instruction.

The black church must never resort to preaching only salvation in the world to come. People are not only asking, "Will there be life after death?" They want to know "Will there be life after birth, and what kind of life will our children have after birth?" Think about it. Will there be life after birth?

Such concerns should stir the total black church family. The black church must promote more lay involvement. The pastors cannot cover all fronts; lay people are needed who will move to Christianize the business, political, and academic structures of society.

Too many lay people are a part of the "black bourgeoisie" or the "black country club." They are also guilty of the sins which they accuse the white man of possessing.

As a black preacher, I must not only be happy with praying beautiful prayers at civic gatherings but must be even more concerned about pricking the consciences at civic gatherings.

Wherever wrong reaches out for justice, wherever the poor seek jobs and food, and wherever victims of prejudice cry out of their hurt, the church must be there—because Jesus is there.

While preaching nonviolence to black youth, the black church must educate white Christians about the ugly monster of velvety violence which is legalized by white power. This violence is the refusal to train and employ blacks; it is the unwillingness to admit blacks into union apprentice programs. Legalized white violence, though kind and polite, is sinful. It is the manager of the "no down payment" stores that charge many times the original price for the cheapest product; the rundown and rat-infested shacks; and the overcrowded and neglected all-black schools that intellectually kill would-be George Washington Carvers at an early age.

If the black church is to have a worthwhile future, it must redefine theological concepts, like sin, into concrete, experiential language. The children of the devil become the narcotic pushers or the pimps. Those who perpetrate crime in the ghetto are killers, children of the night, and workers of iniquity.

Youth who disrupt classrooms, refusing to learn and preventing others from learning, and youth who see the sacred as profane are among the lost; and rather than condemn them, we must help them find salvation. Black youth who condemn the white man for exploiting black women in slavery must not be guilty of sexual brutality and immature exploitation of our daughters, sisters, and wives.

The black church must remain true to the gospel of Jesus Christ. When we study the message of our Lord, we discover that we *are* somebody. We learn that we *have worth* and are a beautiful people. We learn that we are the sons of God.

Because of Jesus, we learn that we can live in peace with our God, with ourselves, and with our fellow man.

We are no longer ashamed of our blackness. Our experiences as Christian black men have taught us to identify with the wretched poverty class of the third world countries of Asia, Africa, and Latin America. We cannot forget the hungry of India, the diseased of Africa, the war weary of Vietnam, the peasants of Mexico and Peru, and the white, poverty-ridden families of the Ozarks. We love the homeless Arabs and the persecuted Soviet Jews.

We know that Jesus is calling us. We have heard him call us to service. He tells us to finish the work he started. He gave sight to the blind. He bound up broken hearts. He set the prisoners free. He preached Good News to the poor. Will we follow him? What is our future? Where are we going? Will we be obedient to him who is calling us? Can we move forward, praying:

God of our weary years,
God of our silent tears,
Thou who hast brought us thus far on the way.

Thou who hast by Thy might
Led us into the light,
Keep us forever in the path, we pray;

Lest our feet stray from the places, our God, where we met Thee,
Lest, our hearts drunk with the wine of the world, we forget Thee.

Shadowed beneath Thy hand,
May we forever stand
True to our God, true to our native land!

"Negro National Anthem," James Weldon Johnson

James H. Stewart is presently the pastor of McGee Avenue Baptist Church in Berkeley, California. He is a member of the Alameda County Welfare Commission, a board member of OIC, and a board member of the American Baptist Churches of the West. He is president of the Northern California Ecumenical Council Table and adjunct professor at the Pacific School of Religion, Berkeley, California. He holds a Bachelor of Arts degree from San Francisco State College; and a Master of Divinity degree from the American Baptist Seminary of the West, Covina, California. He also attended the Seattle Pacific College Graduate School of Business.

The Cost of Citizenship

James H. Stewart

They had listened to him until he said this, but now they raised a great shout,

"Kill him, and rid the earth of such a man! He is not fit to live!"

As they were yelling and ripping their clothes and hurling dust into the air, the colonel gave orders to bring Paul into the barracks and directed that he should be examined by scourging, so that he might discover the reason for such an uproar against him. But when they had strapped him up, Paul spoke to the centurion standing by,

"Is it legal for you to flog a man who is a Roman citizen, and untried at that?"

On hearing this the centurion went in to the colonel and reported to him, saying,

"Do you realize what you were about to do? This man is a Roman citizen!"

Then the colonel himself came up to Paul and said,

"Tell me, are you a Roman citizen?"

And he said,

"Yes."

Whereupon the colonel replied,

"It cost me a good deal to get my citizenship."

"Ah," replied Paul, "but I was born a citizen."

Then those who had been about to examine him left hurriedly, while even the colonel himself was alarmed at discovering that Paul was a Roman and that he had had him bound (Acts 22:22-29, Phillips).

One of the obvious points of tension in our society and the world today is racial unrest, an unrest which stems from a number of factors, not the least being the concept of neocolonialism; Saul Alinsky calls it a "zoo keeper mentality" on the part of the dominant group. In America we have experienced a kind of neocolonialism; therefore, I elected to direct my comments to the subject of citizenship. The crux of the racial problem is centered around the idea of whether or not there will be two classes of citizenship—first and second, preferred and deferred. Thus, the Roman soldier's words to Paul provoke thought pertinent to our present plight—"It cost me a good deal to get my citizenship." What had it cost him? Why should some pay for what others are born into?

Racism is exhibited in many forms, conscious and unconscious. But perhaps no greater evidence exists than that which comes via inordinate national pride and position. A preferred position held at the expense and exclusion of fellow human beings is one definition of institutionalized white racism. For years, multitudes of nonwhites (blacks especially) have been decrying their status as second-class citizens, a condition which denied both voting privileges in some sections of the country and public accommodations in others, as well as allowing faulty hiring practices in all areas of America. Such conditions, the heritage of a heinous slave society, have produced the present tensions and racial unrest tearing at the seam of our nation's garment—a fabric weakly woven on the looms of lust and which threatens to unravel and leave us naked before the eyes of the world. So volatile has this strife been that few are unaware of the Kerner Report, which stresses our heading for two societies: one black, one white, separate and unequal. "What hope is there," as Meridian Henry puts it in James Baldwin's play *Blues for Mister Charlie,* "for a people who deny their deeds and disown their kinsmen and who do so in the name of purity and love, in the name of Jesus Christ? What a light, my Lord, is needed to conquer so mighty a darkness!"[1] Does one even dare to hope, especially in the light of statements such as those made by Price M. Cobbs, coauthor of *Black Rage,* in Seattle, Washington, in 1969, as a speaker for the Human Relations Council: "There will be no more black sacrifices on the altar of white racism. It is too great a price to ask any one group to pay for what is their God-given right"? Our citizenship has cost us in some instances our lives— witness the deaths of Medgar Evers, Jimmy Lee Jackson, Cheney, Schwerner, Luizzo, and Reeb. Some black lives and a few white lives have been lost. It has cost us our cultures inasmuch as integration in America means that the dominant group absorbs minorities and the price we pay is to become white. Many of us are at present going through an identity crisis. The dashikis and Afro hairstyles are attempts to say who we are as black Americans of African descent, even as the Indians (who are perhaps the most preyed upon people at this moment) are attempting to establish their identity.

From across our nation, brown, yellow, black, red, and, yes, poor whites are racially discriminated against because they are forced to pay an inequitable price for citizenship. Interestingly enough, the cost of citizenship to the major group has been the cost of conscience, which is, obviously, also a great price to pay. Slavish structuring of

[1]James Baldwin, *Blues for Mister Charlie* (New York: The Dial Press, 1964), p. 77.

the status quo has fostered South African apartheid industrial relations, South American slave wages for Indians, and an unjustifiable interference in the internal affairs of Vietnam. Job asked the question a long time ago, which needs to be restated and reassessed: "Shall I offer the fruit of my loins for the sin of my soul? God forbid!" I'm not certain of all that Patrick Henry had in mind when he made his historic statement:

> Is life so dear, or peace so sweet, as to be purchased at the price of chains . . .? Forbid it, Almighty God! I know not what course others may take, but as for me, give me liberty, or give me death![2]

We have fought America's wars from Bull Run to Pork Chop Hill. We've been used, abused, and misused, and never could we be labeled traitor. Nisei (Japanese Americans), to the eternal shame of white America, were herded into concentration camps during World War II, had their property confiscated (much of which was never restored), and yet their young men won more Purple Hearts for exemplary service than any other single group. What has been required of some as the cost of citizenship is too great a price to pay for what in the Christian faith purportedly is God's design—neither Jew nor Greek, bond nor free, but all one in Christ Jesus.

One of the great sources of pride an older acquaintance of mine had was his grandfather's freedman's papers, or manumission papers, which declared to all men that he had worked (in excess of his regular labors) and bought his freedom. When a person pays for something so dear at so great a price, he's not likely to regard it lightly. There is a great deal of speculation as to why this soldier in our Scripture text intervened in this attempt to have the apostle Paul flogged. Let's attribute to him some lofty ideals and say that because of what he understood being a citizen of Rome to mean, he was protecting Paul's rights as a Roman. Quite obviously, being a Roman entitled one to certain protection by the law. This is implied in Paul's question, "Is it lawful for you to scourge a man that is a Roman, and uncondemned?" (Acts 22:25, KJV). Just prior to this, in Acts 21:39, Paul had requested permission to address a crowd in Jerusalem on the basis of being a Jew of Tarsus and a citizen of no mean city. Thus, we see Paul claiming the right to be heard and protesting any act of interference. Significant of our age are the voices of countless numbers of

[2]John Bartlett, *Familiar Quotations,* 13th ed. (Boston: Little, Brown and Company, 1955), p. 369.

minorities who are contending for the right of redress for countless wrongs committed against them. For these contentions, reprisals in the form of economic deprivation, denial of citizenship rights, and physical abuse have been the consequence. Still, such reprisals have failed to dissuade the dissenters who protest second-class citizenship. The cost alone is not in terms of the toll it has taken on its victims, but what it costs the country in terms of productivity and creativity. But while citizenship rights seem desirable, no system can command or exact allegiance that subordinates human rights and, above all, ultimate loyalty to God. Christians are citizens first of the kingdom before they have any sacrilegious subscription to any earthly system. Anything that denies justice and rights to any citizen ought to be suspected and questioned by all—especially the people of God. One of the things for which Branch Rickey, now departed Methodist layman and famous baseball figure, is remembered is opening major league baseball to blacks. Jackie Robinson was the first. What I remember are Rickey's words about baseball, what it had meant to him and what it had given him in terms of happiness. Then he said, "I couldn't die and face my God knowing that I had denied to any man that which has meant so much to me." What the cost was to Rickey I don't know, but I don't think he suffered as a consequence of his actions. Still, as God's people, our contending for right will not be without some hazard to self.

The cost of citizenship is the price one pays for the qualities of life which, according to one of our documents, are inherent rights, the God-given rights of all. Said price being the willingness to suffer.

What it has cost and is costing the nation needs to be examined as to its worth—riots, burnings, etc.—but the loss of some real estate is hardly the most critical outcome. Rather, it is the polarization described in the Kerner Report, depicting the two separate societies. The question is: can those of primary group status allow this to occur with the full knowledge of the too great cost to nonwhites?

Paul's persecution was stopped because he claimed his rights as a Roman. Racism's roots go deep, due to inordinate regard for the good of some and disregard for the good of others. Its cure? Sarah Patton Boyle, author of *The Desegregated Heart,* in her book *For Human Beings Only* says,

Integration is upon us—upon those who wish it and those who do not. The task now is to make it work. This will not be easy, yet it can be done if many firm bridges of individual fellowship reach out across the canyon of misinterpretation which divides our land. . . .

Integration can be made to work because it must. Here lies the one hope for us all. Our divisions in America are only the world's divisions in miniature. If we learn to create an indivisible nation, we can move toward creation of an indivisible world.

Surely all can now see that time has run out. Either we quickly move toward the brotherhood of all men or there will not be any men.[3]

[3]Sarah Patton Boyle, *For Human Beings Only* (New York: The Seabury Press, Inc., 1964), pp. 12-13. Copyright © 1964 by Sarah Patton Boyle. Used by permission of The Seabury Press, Inc.

Robert Colby Thomas, now deceased, was pastor of the Church of All Faiths in Oakland, California. He also had been a lecturer at California State University at Hayward, California, and an adjunct professor at San Francisco Theological Seminary at San Anselmo, California. He earned his B.A. from Leland College, his M.R.E. from Golden Gate Theological Seminary, and his D.Min. from San Francisco Theological Seminary. He also attended the University of Denver; San Francisco State University; Pacific School of Religion, Berkeley, California; and Perkins School of Theology, Dallas, Texas. He had been active in the civil rights movement and in community affairs, receiving the National Lane Bryant Award for Outstanding Community Leader in Oakland, California. He wrote and coordinated special summer youth programs in that community and was the president of the anti-poverty board as well as board director and county trustee in several other community organizations.

The Gateway to Life

Robert Colby Thomas

My subject is not the majestic Golden Gate Bridge, often acclaimed as the Gateway to the East, but "The Gateway to Life." "As you exercise these qualities you will never make a slip" (2 Peter 1:10*b*, Moffatt). Man, because of his fascination and quest for life, has often attempted to define its meaning. For Marcus Aurelius life was but a campaign or course of travels, and after fame, it was oblivion. To Henri Amiel, life was a series of agonies, a Calvary which we can climb only on bruised and aching knees. For Ralph Waldo Emerson life was a series of surprises and was not worth taking or keeping if it were otherwise. For James Russell Lowell life was but the womb wherin we are shaped to be born into the next life. Martin Luther King viewed life as a cause to die for: find the cause and you begin to live. Jesus likened life to a treasure in the field: find it and you find life. But if you have problems relating to the treasure, then "Follow me," said Jesus, "for I am life."

Today, every conceivable medium is directed toward polarizing young minds with secular definitions for life. Tobacco firms overdramatize the pleasure and zest in smoking. National brewers glamorize an assortment of beers with the indictment that you have never lived until you have tasted this or that product of the brewers' art. Men and women who are prostituting the code of ethics and morality are being singled out for special awards and applauded as the symbols of the virtuous life. Perhaps the most influential force on youth today is in the field of entertainment. Now, I am a lover of music and can "dig" most of what's going down today, but I think the theology of some of the contemporary lyrics is poor.

Now, I am not here today to impose any cures or prognosis for this sickening social climate, but I am suggesting that none of you take the next train to Georgia like the dude who decided L.A. was just too much for him. He was disgusted because he had not become a star; so he left town. I don't know how old he was, but I say to you that that is a cop-out, for each of you can be a star right in your own city, if you take seriously the apostle Peter's admonition. You see, Peter was a practical man of action, who was known even then as an activist. Whether fishing or mending nets, whether vigorously professing his loyalty to Jesus (even to death), or taking the sword to defend him in the garden, this man of action was up and doing. In this spirit he seems clothed again with a living, speaking personality, transmitting to each of us the secret of the good life.

Giving all diligence is the first thing suggested for the Christian life. Diligence is a word which elsewhere is translated "haste, carefulness, or business." It is taking advantage of opportunities now that will lead to meaningful fulfillment later. It is the delicate process of adding to religion those elements that will make life viable and creative—alertness, promptness, boldness, and persistence, to list a few.

"Add to your faith virtue" (2 Peter 1:5, KJV). For Peter, faith is more than an intellectual assent to a speculative truth or an historical fact; it is, first of all, an act of loving devotion to a person in answer to God's claims upon the heart and his manifold love of grateful devotion; it is, in fact, faith in Christ. Such a faith means having a vision of Christ's perfection, yes, but also of what you, too, can become. Even the black boy, Stevie Wonder, sings about a boy born in hard-times Mississippi, surrounded by four walls; even this child of poverty can make it with a faith and vision in God. Then, such a faith also means aspiration, which suggests that we have a passion to seek the qualitative life. It is a restless kind of faith that will not content itself with marginal living and mediocrity. It is a faith graphically described by Dr. Benjamin Mays as that which causes a person to set his sights for a distant, mountaintop challenge only to hear, once he has reached that lofty goal, another call coming from a higher plateau, saying, "You have not arrived yet; come up a little higher." And faith means transformation, or change. Someone has said there is nothing more constant than change itself. Don't be carried away by those who contend that the God of Judeo-Christianity is obsolete and irrelevant, and don't defect to some mystic cult, for we do not need a new God to have faith in but rather a new faith in the same God. We need faith for these changing times. Peter reminds us to supply our faith with virtue, for it is the energy of God. Although virtue is translated from the Greek as "excellence," I like the Latin derivative, meaning the quality of manhood or heroism. It is the special quality of life without which a man is merely a creature, an animal. It gives tone and dignity and force to men. Virtue and manliness are almost synonymous. The ten golden virtues mentioned in the Bible are charity, chastity, continence, courage, excellence, faith, hope, justice, prudence, and fortitude. But virtue must have in it a supply of knowledge, so Peter adds to virtue knowledge. Knowledge means insight and understanding; it means wide acquaintance with the truth; it means a well-instructed mind.

This knowledge covers three relations of life: God, neighbor, and self. A deeper knowledge of God will result in a fuller knowledge of our relationship to neighbor and self. Other groups are making inroads into our congregations today because they have teaching-oriented programs designed to equip followers in the knowledge of God. You will need this knowledge to guide you as you face the uncertain adversities of life. But with all of your getting of knowledge, remember that knowledge without common sense is folly.

And to knowledge add temperance. The best word for it is self-control, the grace of abstaining from all kinds of evil to which you are tempted, of holding back when lust urges you to go forward. It implies that the man who is truly temperate has the faculties of his mind, as well as his constitutional propensities, under the most complete command. He is like the managed steed in the hand of the rider, like the helm in the hand of a steersman; he is strong and steady; his tongue, his temper, his very thoughts are under authority; and instead of being run away with and rendered ridiculous by his own wayward passions, he, by his strong will, is ever able to subdue the whole body.

And to temperance add patience. The word classically means remaining behind, either taking or being forced to take the hindermost place, being compelled to stand still when you desire to go forward. No discipline can be imagined more severe for the average, restless, human character. While temperance is the grace of holding back, patience is the grace of holding on. The Revised Standard Version translates it as steadfastness. Peter intentionally lists patience this far down in the order of Christian growth because it is a quality appertaining only to an advanced stage of spiritual development. A patient person is rare. Job has been called the most patient of men; but even Job—under the torment of his painful disease, under the wrongheaded argumentation of his friends, under the nagging of his wife—lost self-control and cursed the day he was born. Someone has suggested that there are three stages in the exercise of patience. First, it is simply submission to the will of God when in the midst of disappointment or suffering; second, it expresses itself in persistent endurance; and third, its active quality is shown in faith in God and in a forward view. It was this kind of patience that gripped Dante, whose heart was charged with public sorrow and private suffering, and yet he wrote his *Divine Comedy*. It was in the shadow of threatening death that Mozart composed his immortal *Requiem*. John Milton's youth was marked by flashing brilliance, but his literary masterpiece dates from his later years that were darkened by blindness. Submission, perseverance, and faith—master these, and you qualify among the rare breed of the patient.

And add to patience godliness. Godliness is faith alive and active, not only looking and thinking but also feeling, speaking, and doing, thus infusing into all outward and visible performance a moral element that makes virtue holiness. Godliness is piety in the best sense of the word; fidelity to natural obligations, such as parents, dutifulness in religion, and devoutness. This is not a sentimental and emotional religiosity; rather, it is a strong awareness of the God-relatedness of all life. It is that attitude which sees all things in their relation to God and receives all things from God. There are three words which, taken separately, will give you some idea of the fullness of the grace of godliness: reverence, loyalty, and godlikeness. Here, Peter reminds us that we are the children of the Highest, and our conceptions of the new life—its scope and scale, its relations and responsibilities—must necessarily be embodied in conduct. We cannot live our new life nobly unless we think of it grandly. And we must remember our high origin if we would not fail our great destiny.

And with godliness one needs brotherly kindness, or affection. It is best expressed as a love for the brotherhood, the household of faith. In love of the brethren there are no distinctions and no partiality—no big "I's" and little "you's." It is a love that loves for love's sake alone. It seeks no praise or acclaim; it loves because its nature is love; it loves because God is love. It is a love that is not localized to the members of this or that church but a love that reaches out to the community.

Finally, brotherly affection must flow into love. Love here signifies universal love, the love of humanity. Lest the love of the brotherhood be limited to those within this sacred enclosure, Peter directs that it flow beyond these walls. Love here is the real and final thing; it is love for all men. It never asks the question, "Who is my neighbor?" but asks, "How can I show myself neighborly?" Love does not inquire, "Whom ought I to help?" Rather, it inquires, "How can I best be a helper?" Love is the root of roots, the seed of seeds, the sap of saps, the juice of juices. Love is the electrical current of the soul. Love is the first and the last. When I have love, I have everything; without love I am nothing. Love is all faith, all hope.

This, dear friends, is the gateway to life. I challenge you to pass through it in your quest for life, remembering that this is a great time to be alive, for there are still hidden treasures undiscovered; there are songs yet to be written, books yet to be printed; there are inventions yet to be created, reservoirs of knowledge yet untapped; there are seas still unexplored, and highways where men's feet have never trod. Yes, there are mountains never scaled, diseases still unconquered, problems still unsolved, knowledge that still mystifies, and a God yet to be fully understood.

Harry S. Wright is the pastor of Cornerstone Baptist Church, Brooklyn, New York. Previously he was dean of the chapel of Bishop College, Dallas, Texas, and minister of the Shiloh Baptist Church in Bennettsville, South Carolina. He also has been a lecturer for the General Division of the National Sunday School and B.T.U. Congress. A native of South Carolina, he received his A.B. degree from Morehouse College, Atlanta, Georgia; his B.D. degree from Colgate Rochester Divinity School; and his S.T.M. degree from Perkins School of Theology, Dallas, Texas.

Rules for the Road

Harry S. Wright

I want to read a few words from the lips of a man who has found a way to keep his feet firmly planted on the ground of reality, one who has found joy that brings into his life both light and life, one who has discovered something that holds him steady and brings him through. He begins with a question directed straight to the young:

> How shall a young man steer a [steady]
> course?

His answer to this good question follows in the same breath:

> By holding to thy word.
> I treasure thy promise in my heart,
>   for fear that I might sin against thee.
> Thy word is a lamp to guide my feet
>   and a light on my path;
> I have bound myself by oath and solemn vow
>   to keep thy just decrees.
>   (Psalm 119:9, 11, 105-106, NEB)

The late Ozora S. Davis made several statements that were shocking in their prophetic boldness. He said:

Nobody breaks the rules of God and gets away. Nobody breaks the Ten Commandments; they break you. Nobody disregards the rules of a moral universe with impunity. We disregard these at our own peril. Disobey the moral expectations of a moral universe—run roughshod through the moral landscape of youth, and you will wreck. Drive through the "redlights" in a moral universe at your own risk. We do not break the rules; they break us . . . get by maybe, but never away.[1]

Joe Louis, "The Brown Bomber," in his return match with the great German boxer Max Schmeling, was heard to whisper in the ears of his challenger during a clinch: "You can run, but you can't hide. There is no hiding place in this ring."

The Bible, especially the Wisdom Books, directs its attention to us, the young. These Scriptures share the sober experiences of the aged.

---

[1]Ozora S. Davis, "The High Cost of Low Living," *Out for Character* (Philadelphia: The Vir Publishing Co., 1922), pp. 108, 109.

They pass along to us the crystallized concensus of those who have accumulated wisdom along life's tedious journey. They contain the distilled deposits of wisdom about God, life, human conduct, and which routes and highways through life are safest and best. Over and over again in these sober convictions of human experience there is the warning about the suggested rules:

Obey these timeless rules, and live. Disregard these rules, and you travel at your own moral risks.

I make an indirect plea for "safe driving"; but I make a direct plea for "safe living." What this ancient sage says about the straight path and lamps for the feet and light for days to come are at least worth hearing about, for the psalmist is convinced, and so am I, that there is law and order in the universe.

There is much disorder about us. One need only look in any quarter to find evidences of disarray. About us is economic disorder. About us is political, racial, and international disorder among groups, races, and nations. There are times when I agree with the thinking of many of you that it appears all of the rules, regulations, signposts, and guidelines have been swept away by the tumult and pressures of our time.

But I am convinced that all of the signs are not down. I am convinced that all directives are not awash in the sea of moral relativity. All rules are not caught in the undertow of change; nor are all of the guidelines blown over by the gale winds of a world Nathan Scott calls *The Broken Center*. He says, "[Ours is] an age when all is in doubt and when, as Yeats says, 'things fall apart' and 'the center cannot hold.'"[2]

There is law and order in the universe. There are *rules for the road* which can plant our feet on firm ground for living and bring us through. There are signs yet erect which can steady our course. There are words of reality which can provide instant light and lift for our immediate pathways; and there is a reality which can offer a beam of light down the corridors of our uncertain tomorrows.

The writer of the psalm said it: "Thy word have I hid in mine heart, that I might not sin against thee. Thy word is a lamp unto my feet" (KJV). This promise of a lamp for the feet is our promise of immediate and instant light and lift. This is existential, practical, and immediate. "Thy word is a light on my path." This light for the path is

[2]Nathan A. Scott, Jr., *The Broken Center* (New Haven: Yale University Press, 1966), p. 2

a promise for hope in which to hope. This is eschatological and futuristic and promises light and life for days to come.

And now I want to make three specific suggestions of "Rules for the Road" on which you travel:

(1) Watch your lane.

(2) Mind your speed.

(3) Pull over occasionally and rest; think and reflect on things lasting.

I would like to invite, challenge, and caution you to be yourself. Watch the lane of life in which you travel and spend your days. Mind the "groove" you choose to express what is in you. You will need to watch *that your lane of traffic is not chosen for you.* The pathway of your days must not be selected by the drumbeats of majorities or minorities, or by the sound of feet of heavy battalions. Carve out a lane, and choose a pace for yourself which will bring out what is high and noble in you.

Most of you have great hopes and prayers riding on your shoulders. Every day and night great drops of sweat and sacrifice fall into the bosom of Mother Nature as an investment in your future. *Please do not lose these hopes.* Peer pressure is a source of great academic and moral casualty. How many fine and promising young people topple over and become moral casualties to be piled high on life's scrap heaps because they are not able to resist the pressures of peers who would have them drive in their lanes!

There are persons who have great dreams. These will inspire, challenge, and bring out what is best in you. There are also persons who drift with the tide and travel with the herd. There are those who spend their days hoping that success and greatness are contagious and that some of the fallout will fall on them. Some wait for something to turn up or hope to "bump" into greatness by accident. Also, there are those who are great lovers of truth, searchers after wisdom, and who have great reservoirs of knowledge with which to challenge you. Find these. Search after these. Choose your lane and pace under the inspiration of their spirits. They will "turn you on." These will "blow your minds" and "light your fires." But there are others who, if allowed, will become portions of your problems rather than portions of your solutions.

Peer pressure is the source of much academic and moral casualty. You find yourself a lane, a "groove," a posture, a stance, a style of living that will express not the worst but the best in you. Do not surrender the choice of your destiny into the hands of anyone. You choose your lane of traffic. You set your pace and speed, remembering that lanes can easily become ruts; and ruts have a way of becoming graves.

I say again, this is a world of law and order. The universe in which we live, contrary to all negative appearances, is one of cosmic unity. The universe is not without a superintendent. There are rules for life. There is ground on which we can stand to find firm footing for a steady course. But there are rules which apply and which must be heeded:

> The body has its physical limitations.
> Nature has firm regulations that are not open
> for debate.
> Guard your lane of traffic.
> Watch your speed. Check the pace of your living.

Try not to speed through these days of your youth and run the risk of burning up and burning out too early. Choose a pace too rapid, and you will never hold out. There are an alarming number of young people in our day "blowing their fuses" and living as if time is going out of style. You miss so much scenery along life's highway when you live at full throttle. The risks are high:

> You can "blow your physical fuses."
> You can short-circuit your mind.
> You can crowd and rush your days.
> You may not be around to draw your social security.

If you can decide on your own lane of traffic for the living of these days and keep "cool on the inside" while others about you lose their heads, you'll be a lady and you'll be a man. And in addition, you will heed the teachings of the Great Master, when he said:

"Enter by the narrow [path]. The [road] is wide that leads to perdition, there is plenty of room on that road, and many go that way; but the [road] that leads to life is small and the road is narrow, and those who find it are few" (Matthew 7:13-14, NEB).

The straight road—the narrow way and steady course—provides light traffic; but it leads home. The broad way through life—the turnpike, the freeway—is well lighted, broad with heavy traffic and lots of gay company; but it leads to wailing and gnashing of teeth. What a short walk it is from what may appear in our youthful days to be stylish, in vogue, and cute to the other side of the street of "salty tears"!

94

John Jasper, perhaps the greatest of all of the black preachers, entitled one of his classic sermons "The Black Diamond Express." He pictured through his inventive imagination this express train of life running daily between earth and hell. He described the thirteen stops this fast express made every twenty-four hours, picking up additional human cargo. He said that this train always arrived with its loads of wasted lives ahead of time. Imagine that! An express train, loaded, making thirteen stops, and yet arriving at its destination not *on* schedule but *ahead of* schedule!

Check your speed once in a while, and be sure that you are not running too fast. Watch your lane occasionally, and be sure that your conduct is not decided by majority or minority opinion. Rest, reflect, and think on things lasting.

The route of the cross, the road which the Master demonstrated for us, may not be life's most scenic route in terms of how the world defines "proper scenery"; but it is firm and safe. And you know what? Those who choose this road and decide to follow the rules for this road do not have to make this trip by themselves. This is worth celebrating: namely, that our strivings can be supported with divine strength.

Let me close with this personal illustration. During the Easter holiday of 1953 I left Rochester, New York, en route to my home in Bennettsville, South Carolina. I was driving a 1935 Ford. It was my first car—old, well worn, but paid for. With excitement I began driving south on Route 15. At Harrisburg, Pennsylvania, I left Route 15 and entered the Pennsylvania Turnpike. Cruising smoothly in the far right lane at forty-five miles per hour, I was tempted to increase my speed and move into the middle lane with the faster traffic. I did. I pulled out with the heavy trucks, struggled up to sixty-five, and strained for seventy. I then pulled into the far left lane with the large buses and the fastest traffic. Suddenly, the temperature gauge registered danger. Then, rattles were heard from every quarter of the car. Then, the right rear fender, which had been wired together and tightened for the journey, came apart and fell off completely. At this speed and in this lane I was caught in the draft of two huge buses, with an engine overheating and a missing rear fender. I managed to weave my way, with great effort, back into the slower, far right lane and stopped at the first rest exit I saw. I put up the hood of my little Ford and let it cool. I tightened the remaining left rear fender. And then the great revelation struck me: I had been driving in the wrong lane. I was driving too fast. My car was not designed for the pressures and tempo of the Pennsylvania Turnpike. I never would have made it home at that pace and in that left lane. I left the rest stop and resumed my journey homeward—but in the far right lane and at a pace with which I could hold out. I arrived home safely.

Would you really like to make *your* life count? Would you really like to implement the prayers of those who love you? Would you really like to help try and "push the world" closer to the day when the kingdoms of this world will become the kingdom of our Lord and Christ? Okay, play it by the rules. You can drive an honest, pure, clean, and straight course. The psalmist gave directions:

> I treasure thy promise in my heart,
>   for fear that I might sin against thee.
> Thy word is a lamp to guide my feet
>   and a light on my path.